G

Nonprofit Risk Management and Contingency Planning

Nonprofit Risk Management and Contingency Planning

Done in a Day
Strategies

PEGGY M. JACKSON,
DPA, CPCU

WILEY

John Wiley & Sons, Inc.

For general information on our other products and services, or technical support, please
contact our Customer Care Department within the United States at 800-762-2974,
outside the United States at 317-572-3993 or fax 317-572-4002.

Wiley also publishes its books in a variety of electronic formats. Some content that appears
in print may not be available in electronic books.
For more information about Wiley products, visit our Web site at http://*www.wiley.com*.

Library of Congress Cataloging-in-Publication Data:
ISBN-13: 978-0-471-71749-2
ISBN-10: 0-471-79036-2

Printed in the United States of America
10 9 8 7 6 5 4 3 2 1

I dedicate this book to Marilyn Barrett, DPA,
who was my faculty advisor for my master's thesis
at Central Michigan University and a member of
my dissertation committee at Golden Gate University.

Contents

Acknowledgments   **xi**
About the Author   **xiii**

CHAPTER 1   **Introduction**   **1**
Overview   1
   Five Common Myths about Risk Management   2
Basic Assumptions   4
   Board and Senior Management Collaboration   4
   Pre-Session Preparation   5
   Template   5
Overview of the Changes in the Legal
Environment   6
   Whistleblower Protection   7
   Document Management and Preservation Policy   8
   Sarbanes-Oxley Best Practices   9
   Example of State Legislation:
     California's Nonprofit Integrity Act   10
   Bottom Line   12
Summary   12

PART I. RISK MANAGEMENT

CHAPTER 2   **What Is Risk Management?**   **15**
What Is Risk Management?   15
   Risk Management and the Nonprofit's Structure   16
   Risk Management Activities   17
What Is *Not* Risk Management?   19
What Does Real Risk Management Look Like?   21
Value-Added Aspect of Risk Management   23

Risk Management Planning   24
Risk Assessment   25
Common Risk Areas within Nonprofits   25
Implementation of Risk Management Activities   30
How Do You Deal with the Risks Once
You Identify Them?   30
Monitoring for Results: Did the Strategies
Work?   32
Risk Management as an Ongoing Process   33
Scheduling the Next Round of Risk
Management Activities   33
Summary   34

CHAPTER 3   **Using the Risk Management Template**   **35**
Building a Risk Management Plan   37
Goals and Objectives   37
The Nonprofit's Profile   38
Risk Assessment   38
Prioritize the Risks   43
Action Steps for Risk Treatment   45
Simple Metrics to Monitor the Results   47
Timetable for the Next Round of Risk
Management Activities   47
Summary   47

CHAPTER 4   **Done in a Day Session for Risk Management**   **49**
How to Prepare for the DIAD Session   49
Timetable for Preparation   51
The DIAD Session   54
Sample Agenda   55
Sample Format of a DIAD Session   55
Introduction to Risk Management Planning
Training Curriculum Outline   56
Summary Q&A   58
Sample Outline   63
Summary   64

PART II. BUSINESS CONTINUITY PLANNNING

CHAPTER 5   **Business Continuity Planning**   **67**
Two Important Lessons from September 11   67
What Is Business Continuity Planning?   68
Sources of Business Interruptions   71

Crisis Communication Plan 73
It's Just a Matter of Time 74
Nuts and Bolts of an Effective Crisis
Communication Plan 74
Value Proposition of Business Continuity
Planning 76
Preserving Your Nonprofit's Good Name 76
Remaining a Viable Entity 77
Preserving Stakeholder Confidence 77
Lessons Learned from the Private Sector 78
Summary 81

CHAPTER 6 **Using the Business Continuity Planning
Template** **83**
Beginning to Plan: Some Considerations 83
Introducing the Business Continuity
Planning Template 85
Part I Crisis Incident Management 88
Crisis Incident Management Strategies 89
Part II Transitioning from Managing the Crisis
Incident to Resuming Business Operations 99
Establishing a Timetable for Updating the
Business Continuity Plan 108
Summary 108

CHAPTER 7 **Done in a Day Session for Business Continuity
Planning** **109**
How to Prepare for the DIAD Session 109
Timetable Frame for Preparation 112
Nonprofit Operations—Basic Information 116
Don't Reinvent the Wheel—Even Outdated
Plans Can Be Edited 117
The Done in a Day Session 120
Sample Format of a DIAD Session 121
Business Continuity Planning Template 124
Summary 131

PART III. ADDING VALUE TO RISK MANAGEMENT
AND BUSINESS CONTINUITY PLANNING

CHAPTER 8 **Training in Resource Management and Business
Continuity Planning for Staff and Volunteers** **135**
Leveraging Training for Maximum Results 135

Designing a Curriculum That Works   136
Sample Training Agendas and Curricula   138
   Risk Management Training   138
   How You Can Help: Your Role in
     Risk Management   141
Business Continuity Training   141
Hands-on Training Exercises   148
   Nature and Use of Emergency Preparedness
     Exercises   148
   Practice, Practice, Practice   149
   Sample Desktop Exercises   152
   How Is the Success of Emergency Preparedness
     and Desktop Exercises Measured?   156
Summary   157

CHAPTER 9   **The ROI of Risk Management and Business
Continuity Planning**   **159**
Leveraging Risk Management and Business
   Continuity Planning for Greater Effectiveness   159
   How Risk Management and Business Continuity
     Planning Facilitates Compliance in Today's
     New Legislative Environment   162
Leveraging Risk Management and Business
   Continuity Planning to Improve the Quality of
   Form 990 Filings   166
Summary   167

CHAPTER 10   **Ten Ways to Jump-Start the Process**   **169**

Appendix A   **175**

Appendix B   **179**

Bibliography   **193**

Index   **195**

Acknowledgments

I am grateful for the support of my editor, Susan McDermott, and the wonderful team of talented staff in production and marketing at John Wiley & Sons. You are the greatest!

I would also like to acknowledge and thank my colleague, Toni Fogarty, Ph.D., MPH, for her work in helping to refine and present the business continuity planning resources. Our clients benefited greatly from her hard work, dedication and a level of diplomacy that only a native Nashvillian could bring to difficult situations.

I would also like to acknowledge the support and encouragement I continually receive from friends, family and colleagues. Paul, Rick and Jan keep things in humorous perspective. I particularly appreciate the support from my colleagues in the Business Alliance at the San Francisco Chamber of Commerce, my colleagues in the Center City (San Francisco) Chapter of BNI, and from my colleagues in the San Francisco Junior League.

About the Author

Dr. Peggy M. Jackson is a consultant and nationally-recognized lecturer in risk management, business continuity planning and Sarbanes-Oxley compliance. Dr. Jackson has coauthored five books on risk management, and has recently completed her sixth book, *Sarbanes-Oxley for Nonprofits*, co-authored with Toni E. Fogarty, Ph.D., published by John Wiley and Sons. Four (4) new books will be published by John Wiley & Sons in 2006: *Leveraging Sarbanes-Oxley for Small Businesses, Sarbanes-Oxley for Nonprofit Management* (co-authored with Toni E. Fogarty, Ph.D) and *Sarbanes-Oxley for Nonprofit Boards*. She is a partner with Fogarty, Jackson & Associates and a Principal with Adjunct LLC in San Francisco, CA.

Dr. Jackson earned a doctorate in public administration (DPA) from Golden Gate University in San Francisco and holds the professional designation of Chartered Property and Casualty Underwriter (CPCU). She designed the Jackson Risk Management Model© as part of an award-winning doctoral dissertation on risk management techniques.

She is a member of the San Francisco Chamber of Commerce, the Golden Gate Chapter of the Chartered Property and Casualty Underwriters (CPCU) Society, and the San Francisco Junior League. Dr. Jackson is a frequent speaker on risk management and business continuity planning.

Dr. Jackson is also the coauthor (with Toni Fogarty) of *Sarbanes-Oxley and Nonprofit Management: Skills, Techniques, and Methods* (February 2006) and *Sarbanes-Oxley for Nonprofits: A Guide to Building Competitive Advantage* (April 2005), both published by John Wiley & Sons, Inc.

Introduction

OVERVIEW

The news reports are full of stories about nonprofits in trouble. Senator Charles Grassley (R-IA) and the U.S. Senate Finance Committee have held hearings into nonprofit accountability, and Governor Arnold Schwarzenegger of California has signed a bill into law that holds nonprofits accountable for governance, financial, and fundraising activities. Today's legislative expectations have raised the bar for the private sector and the nonprofit sector alike. Nonprofits are being scrutinized at the federal level not only by the Senate Finance Committee, but by the Internal Revenue Service, with greater inspection of 990 forms. The California Nonprofit Integrity Act applies not only nonprofits domiciled in California, but to any nonprofit that solicits donations or otherwise does business in the state.

The nonprofit world's response to these heightened expectations is not always astute. Dean Zerbe, senior aide to Senator Grassley, commented in an interview with the *Chronicle of Philanthropy* that he routinely encounters these three groups of nonprofit people: "[o]striches . . . deny problems; Luddites believe there is no need for change but advocate stiffer enforcement of nonprofit laws; and fig-leaf reformers come up with ideas that appear to offer solutions but actually allow problems to persist" (Wolverton, 2005, p. 38).

How can nonprofits address these changes in requirements and expectations? Risk management and business continuity planning are two techniques that have the potential for facilitating growth and strengthening the internal structure of nonprofits. But as with any good-for-you regimen, there are always plenty of excuses not to engage in these healthy activities.

Five Common Myths about Risk Management

Often nonprofits defer risk management planning because they are apprehensive about beginning the process. Many times this fear stems from five common myths about risk management and business continuity planning:

1. It takes forever.
2. It involves a lot of navel gazing.
3. It will step on toes.
4. The finished plan will have to be at least four inches thick.
5. It gathers dust on the shelf once it is finally completed.

Bonus myth:

6. If we do it right, we can eliminate risk altogether.

Of course, none of these myths is true, but they all are significant in their power to keep nonprofits from engaging in risk management and business continuity planning. The truth about these myths points to the need for nonprofits to take a more streamlined approach to this type of planning:

The Truth

- *It takes forever.* The Done in a Day (DIAD) method of risk management and business continuity planning accelerates the process by allowing for a structured preparation with a concentration of time dedicated to assembling the plan and developing strategies for execution.
- *It involves a lot of navel gazing.* With DIAD, there is no "paralysis by analysis." The preparation time is structured to identify the necessary data, information, and other resources. Decision making is

compressed to focus on what is needed for a specific time frame. Because risk management and business continuity planning follow a recurring course, there will be opportunities in the next scheduled round to review decisions made today.

- *The process will step on toes.* The best interests of the nonprofit and the community it serves trump any individual egos. The nonprofit's insurance professional, insurance carrier, auditor, banker, and legal counsel will be pleased that the organization has committed to this type of planning.

- *The finished plan will have to be at least four inches thick.* Not using today's technology! An effective risk management plan and/or business continuity plan can fit into the memory of a PalmPilot or BlackBerry. Because one of the themes of DIAD is "less is more," planners focus on the *important* information. The plan must always be user-friendly because staff and volunteers will be expected to fully understand how to participate in its execution.

- *It gathers dust on the shelf once it is finally completed.* Absolutely not! Risk management and business continuity planning need to be woven into everyone's job description and performance objectives. These plans can also serve to strengthen internal controls and facilitate the implementation of Sarbanes-Oxley best practices.

Bonus myth:

- *If we do it right, we can eliminate risk altogether.* Risk can never be eliminated—all of life is a risk. The intent of risk management is to recognize that risks can be neutralized to some extent so that the frequency and severity of losses can be managed.

Despite seemingly nonstop scandals that have affected nonprofits, many leaders are committed to making their nonprofits stronger and more viable entities. Done in a Day planning for risk management and business continuity can serve to build and strengthen their organizations.

An important assumption in this book is that *nonprofits are businesses.* The nonprofit sector is an industry in its own right. Nonprofits' identity of "not for profit" lies solely in their tax classification of 501(c) (3, 4, or whatever). Nonprofits do not stay in operation very long if they lose money. The business models of private companies and nonprofit organizations are more closely aligned today than ever before. Public sector expectations of accountability apply to private companies and nonprofits, as evident from the findings of Senator Grassley's hearings in 2004 and 2005 on nonprofit accountability. Many nonprofits have "for-profit" subsidiaries or related operations, such as ownership of commercial property. Private companies routinely partner with nonprofits on contractual ventures or as part of corporate philanthropy.

This book sets on a mission to:

- Explain what risk management and business continuity planning are and how this type of planning can add value to a nonprofit.

- Illustrate why these plans are *essential* to your nonprofit in today's business environment.

- Describe the most efficient and cost-effective ways to design and execute these plans.

- Present risk management and business continuity planning templates to facilitate the design of the first edition of your nonprofit's plans.

- Show how risk management and business continuity planning can help your nonprofit come into compliance with Sarbanes-Oxley legislation and state legislation, such as California's Nonprofit Integrity Act.

- Present methods to add further value to your planning, such as offering training to your staff and leveraging planning for competitive and marketing advantage.

BASIC ASSUMPTIONS

Board and Senior Management Collaboration

Before you begin a DIAD plan, we should review some basic assumptions. The most important assumption is that the nonprofit's board and senior management are fully committed to providing the time, space, and resources to the staff and volunteers who are constructing the plan. The board needs to hold itself and senior management accountable for contributing to the plan in terms of new methods and policies. The board and senior management also need to commit to being visible in modeling the desired behavior and practices that are associated with risk management and business continuity planning.

Pre-Session Preparation

The DIAD plans can be completely assembled in one day with some preparatory work in the two to three weeks prior. The preparatory work is essential to the success of the DIAD session. However, it is important to complete the preparatory work quickly and not engage in paralysis by analysis. If your team wants to construct the plan in one day, then you need to commit to completing the (not complex) prep work prior. Chapters 4 and 8 provide detailed descriptions of the preparation methods and include checklists and timelines to simplify the process. The chapters include practical advice for dealing with risks and developing strategies for resuming business operations.

Each DIAD session presumes that your nonprofit has assembled a team to do the preparatory work and to assemble the plan. The team should be large enough to complete the preparatory work in a short time, but not so large as to bog down decision making. The team can be comprised of staff, volunteers, and/or board members—whatever works for your nonprofit. All of the staffing and preparatory work suggestions are just that—suggestions. It is important that your nonprofit put together a team that works for your organization and does the prep work that is relevant to the needs of your organization. The preparatory work and the structure of the plan are intended to be generic and user-friendly so they can be tailored to meet the needs of nonprofits of all sizes.

Template

The DIAD method uses templates as basic tools. Using a template to begin your nonprofit's risk management or business continuity planning is an important way to jump-start the planning process by eliminating the need to design a structure for the plan. The template is a fill-in-the-blanks tool that can be used to design the first edition of your nonprofit's risk management or business continuity plan. If your team decides it would like a different structure for the second round, great! At least your risk management or business continuity planning process has been launched, and your team has had the experience of a round of risk management planning. You can customize the generic components of the template to meet the structural needs of your nonprofit. If some aspect of the template does not apply to your organization, you can simply ignore it.

OVERVIEW OF THE CHANGES IN THE LEGAL ENVIRONMENT

In order to design effective risk management and business continuity plans, planners need to be conscious of the changes in the legislative environment at the federal and state level. These requirements, best practices, and expectations need to be built in to risk management and business continuity plans and will be highlighted in the discussions of plan content.

The Public Company Accounting Reform and Investor Protection Act, commonly referred to as Sarbanes-Oxley (SOX) after its sponsors, Senator Paul Sarbanes (D-MD) and Representative Michael Oxley (R-OH), was passed in 2002 in the wake of the Enron corporate scandal. Although SOX initially was intended to raise the bar for integrity and competence for publicly traded companies, its effect has been to promote greater accountability within both the nonprofit and the private sector.

Currently, only two of the provisions in SOX apply directly to nonprofit organizations. Nonprofits are required to adhere to "whistle-blower protection," which provides protection to employees who report suspected fraud or other illegal activities. Employees or volunteers of a nonprofit are shielded from retaliation for making reports of waste, fraud, or abuse.

Nonprofits are also expected to have a fully functioning document preservation policy in place. This policy has two aspects: preservation and archiving of documents for the purpose of timely retrieval and a prohibition against the destruction or falsification of records or documents.

Whistleblower Protection

The first obligation from SOX that applies to all organizations is the requirement for a documented whistleblower protection policy. SOX requires all organizations, including nonprofits, to establish a means to collect, retain, and resolve claims regarding accounting, internal accounting controls, and auditing matters. The system must allow for such concerns to be submitted anonymously. SOX provides significant protections to whistleblowers and severe penalties for those who retaliate against them.

The policies and procedures that a nonprofit develops must contain at least these features:

- There is a confidential avenue for reporting suspected waste, fraud, and abuse.
- There is a process to thoroughly investigate any reports.
- There is a process for disseminating the findings from the investigation.
- The employee or volunteer filing the complaint will not be subjected to termination, firing, or harassment, or miss out on promotion.
- Even if the findings do not support the nature of the complaint, the employee or volunteer who made the complaint will not face any repercussions.

All employees and volunteers should have a copy of the whistleblower policy, and it should be posted in clear view. This policy should also be covered in any orientation or training programs the organization offers for employees and volunteers.

Document Management and Preservation Policy

Document storage and retention is another area within SOX that applies to all organizations. Some key areas for consideration include:

- What documents and records should be preserved and why?
- Are the documents paper only, or are electronic files included? Which ones?
- What about e-mail and instant messaging?
- What are the expectations about the way in which documents are stored or archived and the ability to retrieve documents?
- How long are you supposed to keep these documents?
- Is there a protocol for disposing of documents once their storage time has elapsed?
- When should you not destroy materials?
- How can you make sure that everyone in the nonprofit—staff and volunteers—understands and adheres to these requirements?
- What happens if your nonprofit is in violation?

The executive team must develop a statement that contains these talking points:

- What the document retention policy is—and why it is required by law. It is important that the staff and volunteers understand that document preservation is a component of SOX that applies to all organizations.
- What new procedures emerge from the policy? Staff and volunteers need to understand how to be in compliance, and what specific actions are required.
- What are the obligations of individuals to ensure that your nonprofit is in compliance? Requirements for individual staff and volunteers should be presented in writing. Because this is probably a very new requirement in your organization, the more user-friendly the guidelines, the better.

- What is expected in terms of new behaviors and procedures, and what are the consequences for individual employees and volunteers for failing to adhere to the new procedures? It is particularly important that the executive team be prepared to carry out unpleasant consequences swiftly to send a strong message throughout the organization.

Sarbanes-Oxley Best Practices

SOX best practices are designed to enhance the completeness and reliability of all aspects of your nonprofit's operations. These practices include:

- Audit committee whose role is to oversee the annual audit or financial review (for small nonprofits) and to upgrade the financial literacy of the board of directors
- Enhanced detail and accuracy in the preparation of IRS Form 990
- Improved governance and a nonprofit board that understands its role as ultimately accountable for the actions of the nonprofit and is willing to take steps to enhance professional development for each member
- Conflict of interest policy and code of ethics that facilitates greater focus on decision making for the good of the nonprofit
- Internal controls, particularly as these relate to financial operations, and compliance with all laws and regulations at the federal, state, and local level
- Transparency at all levels of management
- Adherence to policies and procedures—and enforcement

The nonprofit's commitment to adopting and maintaining SOX best practices can be demonstrated in the deliverables of a review of internal controls. The process and outcomes can be used to measure the development of the platinum standard. Compliance cannot simply be a rote operation; the commitment to excellence must transcend all levels of the organization and be evident in all of the operational systems and in the symbiotic relationship that exists among the various systems within the organization.

Example of State Legislation: California's Nonprofit Integrity Act

In addition to federal legislation and regulatory scrutiny, nonprofits can be subject to state legislation even if they are not domiciled in that state. The state of California passed a Nonprofit Integrity Act (SB1262) in 2004 that imposes many of the features of Sarbanes-Oxley legislation on nonprofits with budgets in excess of $2 million operating in that state. Of particular significance is that this law also applies to *any nonprofit that solicits donation in the state of California regardless of where the nonprofit is domiciled.*

Provisions That Apply to Nonprofits with Revenues in Excess of $2 Million

The law has specific provisions that apply to nonprofits with revenues in excess of $2 million. These provisions include:

- Nonprofits will be required to have an annual audit performed by a certified public accountant (CPA) who is "independent," as defined by U.S. Government auditing standards.
- The results of the audit will need to be made available to the public and the State Attorney General.
- Nonprofits will be required to have an audit committee whose membership cannot include staff and must not overlap more than 50 percent with the finance committee. The audit committee can include members who are not on the organization's board of directors.

What This Means for Nonprofits Operating in California

Nonprofits whose revenues exceed $2 million will be required not only to file an annual audit with the Attorney General's office, but will have to demonstrate that the audit was conducted by an auditor who is independent of the organization. The auditor cannot perform any other services for the nonprofit, including tax preparation. Nonprofits covered by this provision of the law will be required to have an audit committee that conforms to the standards described in the law.

To ensure greater accountability in executive compensation, the law requires that the board approve the compensation, including benefits, of the corporation's president or chief executive officer and its treasurer or chief financial officer for the purposes of assuring that their compensation package is reasonable.

The law also requires disclosure of written contracts between commercial fundraisers and nonprofits. These contracts must be available for review on demand from the Attorney General's office. Fundraisers must be registered with the Attorney General's office.

Provisions That Apply to All Nonprofits, Regardless of Size, Operating in California

Nonprofits are required to:

- Make their audits available to the public on the same basis as their IRS Form 990 if they prepare financial statements that are audited by a CPA.

- File at least 10 days before the commencement of the solicitation campaign, events, or other services notice of the campaign/events/services by a "commercial fundraiser for charitable purposes." This time provision is lifted in emergency cases. Each contract must be signed by an official of the nonprofit and include the contract provisions specified in the law.

- For fundraising activities, not misrepresent or mislead anyone about their purpose, or the nature, purpose, or beneficiary of a solicitation. There must be specific disclosures in any solicitation that the funds raised will be used for the charitable purpose as expressed in articles of incorporation or other governing documents. The nonprofit is expected to ensure that fundraising activities are adequately supervised to make certain that contracts and agreements are in order and that fundraising is conducted without intimidation or undue influence.

What This Mean for Nonprofits Operating in California

Nonprofits in California, regardless of their size, need to review their fundraising practices, particularly if some or all of their fundraising is outsourced to commercial fundraising firms. Nonprofits will be liable for abuses by vendors of fundraising services. As a practical matter, boards should insist that due diligence activities be conducted before contracting with any vendor, particularly those providing fundraising services. The California law, however, places strict parameters on third-party fundraising.

Bottom Line

The days of the "mom and pop" nonprofit are over—you have an obligation to your donors, your clients, your board, and your staff to ensure that your organization is in compliance with the relevant provisions SOX legislation (and SB1262 if you operate or solicit donations in California). It's not just a "best practice"—it's the *law*, and it applies to all organizations in this country, including your nonprofit.

SUMMARY

The DIAD concept is predicated on the values that preserve the nonprofit's mission and preserve its resources. Risk management and business continuity planning need not be resource intensive in terms of time, staff, or money. It is important to look on DIAD activities as the launching pad for *ongoing* risk management and business continuity planning. It's *done* in a day, *but not over* in a day.

PART ONE

Risk Management

CHAPTER 2

What Is Risk Management?

People think of [nonprofits] as very nice warm-hearted people who perhaps aren't very business-like in the way we run operations.
—TOM NOLAN, Project Open Hand, San Francisco, CA

Consider this frightening but true story—A prospective client was a very large nonprofit organization whose range of programs was impressive. Although the organization had not experienced any publicly embarrassing incidents, one of the nonprofit's external advisors was concerned about the organization's blatant disinterest in engaging in any form of risk management. After an extensive dialogue with a large committee of decision makers, our firm's proposal was declined. When our chief executive officer contacted their primary decision maker, he was told that the organization really didn't want anyone from the outside coming in, even to educate their staff about risk management, because they were concerned what the "outsider" would find.

WHAT IS RISK MANAGEMENT?

The term "risk management" can mean many different things, depending on a number of factors. Businesses and some nonprofits have people on their staff whose title is "risk manager," but in reality the person is in charge of managing the firm's insurance portfolio. Risk management is a dynamic activity, not a static function.

Risk management is the means by which a nonprofit can identify, assess, and control risks that may be present within their board, management, staffing, organizational structure, operations, and relations with the public.

The organization actively pursues risk in its operations by examining the quality of its internal controls, safety, actions of its staff on the job, and behavior of its volunteers in their interaction with staff, clients, or the public. More important, risk management is an *ongoing* activity.

Risk Management and the Nonprofit's Structure

A key objective of any successful risk management program is to have risk management practices become fully integrated into every aspect of the organization. Although every nonprofit is unique, all have four common organizational components: the board, staff (including volunteers), operations, and relations with the public.

Board

Members of the board of directors are the *ultimate authority* in the nonprofit. Recent changes in the legislative environment have reinforced this level of responsibility. Nonprofit boards traditionally have been thought of as a group of good-hearted volunteers, but in today's world, nonprofit boards are expected to take their role to new levels of accountability. Boards are responsible for crafting the procedures, policies, and protocols that ensure the nonprofit is in compliance with federal, state, and local laws and is a going concern.

Staff and Volunteers

Staff and volunteers are the primary resources within any organization. Often money or assets are regarded as the nonprofit's most important resource, however, the nonprofit could not exist without its human capital. We include management in this category as well as other individuals who are associated contractually with the nonprofit, such as consultants and contractors.

Operations

The term "operations" describes what the nonprofit does to provide programmatic services, generate revenue, and execute contracts or other activities that support its mission.

Relations with the Public

The nonprofit exists within a community of clients and the public at large. The nonprofit is permitted to exist through the revenue it generates, such as donations, through its IRS tax-exempt classification, and through its legal filings. If the nonprofit's activities or behavior causes its legal status to be imperiled, then the organization can cease to exist. Even if it is permitted to maintain its legal status, public distrust could dry up donations and permanently damage the nonprofit's good name.

Risk Management Activities

There are three primary activities in risk management: risk assessment, risk management strategy implementation, and monitoring for results (see Exhibit 2.1).

EXHIBIT 2.1 Risk Management: Basic Steps

1. *Risk Assessment*—Risk assessment is the step that determines what risks are present in the nonprofit and the potential severity these risks might bring.

2. *Risk Management Strategy Implementation*—In this step, the risks that are identified in the assessment stage are addressed through one or more of the following risk treatments (see exhibit 2.2):

   - In *avoidance,* the activity or practice is discontinued (not usually a practical option). For a nonprofit, this option would mean discontinuing a program or activity that appears to be presenting an unacceptably high level of risk. Usually this option is not either necessary or desirable.

   - In *retention,* a nonprofit either establishes a restricted fund that would be used to address losses from the risk or significantly raises the deductible on an insurance policy that addresses the risk (i.e., automobile policies).

   - *Modification* is the method that considers how the features of a risk can be changed to reduce the risk's potential for frequency or severity. This option is the way most risks are generally treated. The nonprofit considers ways in which the potential for damage from a risk can be reduced by implementing new procedures, protocols, or better training.

   - The *transfer* option is the means by which the financial aspects of the risk are transferred. This is done in a number of ways, the most common method being the purchase of insurance. Although this option generally is combined with modification, it is by no means an end in itself. Claims can raise insurance premiums significantly, and sometimes, if the number of claims is high, coverage will be cancelled or no longer available. Insurance does not cover other significant expenses, such as a court awarding punitive damages for egregious behavior. Insurance does not cover a nonprofit in such cases.

3. *Monitoring for Results*—It is important to ensure that the strategy chosen in step two is effective. Monitoring for results takes place at a specified time following the implementation of the risk management strategy.

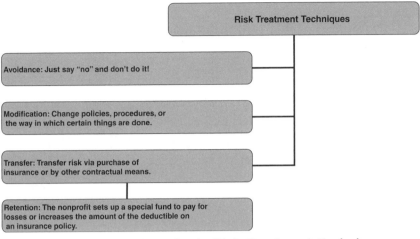

EXHIBIT 2.2 Four Basic Risk Treatment Techniques

Risk management planning is an ongoing activity. Once it is launched via a Done in a Day (DIAD) session, you must schedule future risk management planning rounds. For the first two years, these sessions should take place at least every three to six months. After two years, the planning should take place on an annual or semiannual basis. The regularity of the planning facilitates the continuous examination of risk areas within the four components of the nonprofit:

- Board
- Staff and Volunteers
- Operations
- Relations with the Public

Risk management planning as a routine exercise is a means of identifying new risk areas that have emerged through changes in the organization and its external environment.

WHAT IS *NOT* RISK MANAGEMENT?

The last section reviewed all of the features of risk management and its application in a nonprofit. It is just as important to understand what are *not* risk management activities. These activities do not produce a solid risk management plan that a nonprofit can pursue to reduce the potential for loss or the frequency and severity of accidents or injury:

- *Calling up your agent or broker and purchasing insurance.* Insurance is a method for treating risk, but it is not risk management. If your non-profit sustains too many accidents, injuries, or other reasons to file claims, your insurance policy might be cancelled, or the premium could increase to the point that it is difficult to afford. Insurance covers only certain types of losses and does not cover punitive damages. Further, if your nonprofit has an adverse claims record and your insurance carrier cancels coverage, obtaining replacement coverage may be difficult or impossible.

- *Setting up a committee for endless discussion on the topic.* Nonprofits, in their misguided goal of obtaining consensus on a topic, habitually establish committees to engage in endless "study" or "discussion." A risk management committee that does not deliver a risk management plan and educational piece in a timely fashion is not doing its job. The private sector sets up risk management committees with deadlines and deliverables—and holds people accountable.

- *Buying cheap software that facilitates your denial and enables you to deal with risk issues at arm's length.* This option is particularly attractive to individuals who have no interest in genuine risk management but have been tasked with risk management planning. It is cheap, mindless, and can render a report that will keep senior management off the staffer's case. This option, however, is particularly dangerous in terms of the objectives of good risk management practice. The nonprofit may think it has a risk management plan, but no one other than the person entering the data really has had any contact with it. Cheap software does not educate your nonprofit's management, staff, and volunteers, nor does it help board members to understand what their obligations are in today's post–Sarbanes-Oxley environment. Any product that allows your nonprofit to deal with risk management at arm's length does not provide value for the money.

- *"Playing it by ear" and hoping nothing will happen.* As the song says, "Denial isn't just a river in Egypt." Risk management isn't something that your nonprofit can endlessly "defer" because it just doesn't have the time to deal with it right now. A prospective client once told me that she felt that risk management activities were a "luxury" that took up valuable time which her organization needed for fundraising!

- *Expecting the board to do it first.* The board needs to fully endorse the nonprofit's risk management planning, but the planning process is not contingent on the board doing all of the work.

- *Pleading ignorance: "Our insurance broker didn't tell us we had to do something about risk."* As we saw in the opening story, some nonprofits ignore those professionals who do tell them that they need to engage in risk management activities. Your nonprofit's obligation to engage in such activities stems from its commitment to being true to its mission. No one should have to tell your nonprofit to engage in risk management or business continuity planning—your organization should be eager to embrace this type of planning to ensure its ongoing viability.

WHAT DOES REAL RISK MANAGEMENT LOOK LIKE?

Thus far we have examined examples of the types of activities that are not genuine risk management. How can you tell if a nonprofit has a solid risk management program in place? Here are some clues:

- *Everyone is on the same page.* Everyone in the organization—from the chair of the board to the gardener to the newest volunteer—understands what risk management is and what their role is in the nonprofit's risk management plan. There are rewards for compliance and consequences for failing to comply. The board and senior management model the desired behavior. Staff and volunteers are actively engaged in risk management practices. They are part of the nonprofit's standard operating procedures.

- *It is an ongoing process.* A risk management plan is in place, and risk management planning is an ongoing process with rounds having a three- to six-month cycle. Everyone in the organization has a copy of the current risk management plan, and everyone knows what is expected of him or her.

- *It is important to recognize the value of partnering with the nonprofit's external advisors, such as insurance professionals, finance professionals, and legal counsel.* Real risk management planning includes your nonprofit's insurance, legal, and financial professionals. These professionals must understand your nonprofit and review your risk management plan and provide feedback. The nonprofit works as a partner with these advisors. Risk management practices are fully integrated into the way things are done, the way fundraising is done, the way the board operates, and the way in which the nonprofit works to maintain its good name in the community.

- *Real risk management is holistic, hands-on, and all-inclusive.* Your nonprofit has a plan in place to deal with risks in a comprehensive and coherent fashion; the plan is reviewed regularly; and the nonprofit's insurance broker is a player whose advice and input can be used to leverage the plan for further benefit to the nonprofit. But real risk management does not have to generate paralysis by analysis, nor does it need to be expensive or labor-intensive. Real risk management practice strengthens the nonprofit and provides the solid framework for maintaining financial and organizational viability for decades to come.

These indicators are some examples of the ways in which genuine risk management practices are evident in a nonprofit. Any nonprofit, regardless of its size, can have an excellent infrastructure and a board, management, staff, and volunteer contingent who are committed to making the organization the best it can be.

VALUE-ADDED ASPECT
OF RISK MANAGEMENT

The implementation of a risk management plan can be leveraged with important service providers.

- *Insurance.* Having a risk management plan demonstrates that the nonprofit is committed to being a full partner with their insurance professional in protecting the nonprofit. Insurance companies expect their private sector clients to demonstrate that they are committed to risk management practices. There is no reason why nonprofits should be exempt from this responsibility.

- *Banks and financial institutions.* Banks and other financial institutions want to feel confident in a client before they are willing to offer a loan or line of credit. Your nonprofit's risk management plan is a means by which you can demonstrate to your banker that the organization is committed to solid management practices and is a good lending risk.

- *Remaining in compliance with federal and state law, particularly those requirements to maintain your nonprofit's 501(c)(3).* The legal and legislative environment has changed dramatically in recent years. With the passage of Sarbanes-Oxley Act of 2002, all organizations, including nonprofits, have been obliged to change the way they do business and to accept a higher level of transparency and accountability.

- *Writing proposals for grants.* Funders such as foundations and other institutions are becoming more rigorous in their requirements. Proposals need to include a business plan and should also include the nonprofit's risk management and business continuity plans. Funders are to nonprofits what venture capital firms are to private sector companies. The boards of these organizations want to see results—and want to ensure that funding is going to well-managed organizations.

- *Partnering with other nonprofits or with corporations.* In today's environment, other organizations will want assurances that partnering with your nonprofit does not pose a risk for them. Your non-profit's risk management plan will demonstrate that your organization is committed to solid management practices.

- *Preserving your nonprofit's good name.* Public trust is very fragile. It is intangible but can take years to repair if damaged. One of the challenges in risk management is identifying the ways in which your nonprofit's good name or public image could be damaged. Risk management planning can facilitate important discussions around this topic.

- *Making sure your staff, clients, and volunteers are safe.* A risk management plan can help your nonprofit identify those areas, locations, and situations that might pose danger for your staff, clients, and volunteers. A risk management plan could also establish procedures to keep people safe at special events and fundraisers that the nonprofit presents.

Risk management pays dividends in terms of saving time and money and helping to keep people safe. Chapter 9 addresses the ways in which your nonprofit can leverage your risk management and business continuity plans for competitive and marketing advantage.

RISK MANAGEMENT PLANNING

A risk management plan does not have to be complicated, costly, or labor-intensive, but the plan does need to be consistent in its activities and in the methods for identifying and treating risk. Any risk management plan should incorporate the basic steps of risk assessment, implementation of risk management activities, and monitoring for results.

As your nonprofit begins work on a risk management program, consider what your organization sees as short-term and long-term objectives. These objectives should not be complex, but should be consistent with other goals of the nonprofit in terms of growth, financial objectives, and programmatic expansion. The risk assessment and risk management implementation components of the plan are important in fine-tuning these objectives. As your nonprofit monitors its risk management decisions, it will be able to see if the strategies employed delivered the desired results.

Risk Assessment

The first activity in risk management planning is risk assessment. In risk assessment, the nonprofit evaluates an array of factors that would contribute to its loss history or potential for loss. The factors include the nonprofit's history of claims and accidents, any history of litigation or formal complaints to governmental agencies, and potential for accidents, injuries, or adverse publicity. The nonprofit also needs to examine its level of compliance with federal, state, and local laws and ordinances. The potential for loss needs to be examined in each of the nonprofit's organizational components: the board, staff, operations, and relations with the public.

Common Risk Areas within Nonprofits

Board

The board is the ultimate authority in the nonprofit and ultimately will be held accountable for all actions taken by the nonprofit. Because the board is the entity entrusted with the governance of the nonprofit, the focus of the risk assessment questions and implementation activities centers on defining written standards for behavior and procedures within the board setting. Often the absence of written standards for behavior and procedures leads to practices that could incur liability for the board as a governance entity. The board's fiduciary obligations require very careful oversight of financial operations to ensure that: a budget is crafted on an annual basis; executive compensation is appropriate for the size and mission of the organization; an annual audit or financial review is conducted; and IRS Form 990s are submitted in a timely fashion. The board is responsible for ensuring that all other financial reports are generated in a timely fashion.

The board should ensure that it is in compliance with relevant federal law and regulations, state law and regulations, and any local ordinances. The board should also ensure that documentation of its actions and board minutes are prepared in the appropriate manner and stored per the Sarbanes-Oxley document retention policy.

The board should ensure that human resource policies are in place to safeguard the rights of employees and volunteers and to ensure that every employee and volunteer has a job description and a method by which his or her performance is evaluated appropriately and fairly. The board should also ensure that the nonprofit publishes an employee manual and a volunteer manual that identify and outline policies that apply to employees and volunteers.

The board, as the ultimate authority in the nonprofit, is responsible for ensuring that the nonprofit is adequately insured, including the variety of insurance policies that are required for the nonprofit's operations, professional liability coverage (if applicable), and directors' and officers' insurance, including employment practices liability insurance for the board. The board is also responsible for ensuring that this coverage is secured at a competitive price and that the nonprofit's insurance professional is responsive to the organization's needs and requirements. Term limits are essential for any nonprofit board. Board members need to be transitioned off at regular intervals to keep the board focused, fresh, and independent. One area of particular interest to Senator Grassley and the Senate Finance Committee is the level of independence that a nonprofit board exhibits. The lower the level of independent thinking and action, the more likely that the board will engage in activities that are illegal, unethical, or simply ill-advised.

Board independence has become an integral part of the discussion on overall board accountability. Two or more family members and/or spouses are seated on the board. The independence of individual board members is key to the effective functioning of the board. The presence of family members or spouses as board colleagues interferes with that independence on several levels and is an inherent conflict of interest.

Board members are required to act in accordance with three legal standards: care, loyalty, and obedience. These standards require board members to conduct themselves and board operations in a manner consistent with the legal benchmark of a reasonably prudent person. Board members are obligated to act in accordance with their fiduciary obligations and the mission of the nonprofit. The absence of a conflict of interest policy and/or a code of ethics suggests that the board is either disinterested in its obligations or ignorant of its obligations.

Board meetings must have an agenda and minutes. If they don't, the board really doesn't understand its obligations to the nonprofit, its potential to be held criminally liable for nonprofit mismanagement, and the need for proper documentation of meetings. The entire board of the James Beard Foundation and the entire board of United Way of the National Capital Area were replaced because of scandals at these organizations.

Staff

Human resource management issues are often the most troublesome areas in terms of liability in nonprofit organizations. Issues such as harassment claims, workers' compensation costs, and wrongful termination are consistently reported as significant problems. Volunteers are often ignored in terms of adequate supervision, training, and accountability. If the areas of supervision, job description, and performance reviews are not administered in a manner that can be demonstrated as competent, the nonprofit can incur liability. Background checks, such as of Department of Motor Vehicle or criminal records, must be reviewed carefully for the protection of the nonprofit, its clients, and staff members. Nonprofits must enforce policies and procedures with both volunteer and paid staff. Both types of staff should also have avenues to address grievances and report unsafe conditions.

Risk management activities related to employment issues should include the writing of a personnel policy manual, the drafting of procedures for job reviews, termination, and the handling of grievances. Job descriptions are an essential component in risk management, as these documents provide the parameters for each staff member's responsibilities and accountability and provide proof of his or her responsibilities within the organization.

Sadly, workplace violence, including bomb threats, has become more common. The source of this violence could be a spillover of domestic violence or a disgruntled worker or client.

The Occupational Safety and Health Administration (OSHA) offers this advice:

> Workplace violence is violence or the threat of violence against work-ers. It can occur at or outside the workplace and can range from threats and verbal abuse to physical assaults and homicide, one of the leading causes of job-related deaths. However it manifests itself, work-place violence is a growing concern for employers and employees nationwide.
>
> Some 2 million American workers are victims of workplace vio-lence each year. Workplace violence can strike anywhere, and no one is immune. Some workers, however, are at increased risk. Among them are workers who exchange money with the public; deliver pas-sengers, goods, or services; or work alone or in small groups, during late night or early morning hours, in high-crime areas, or in commu-nity settings and homes where they have extensive contact with the public. This group includes healthcare and social service workers, such as visiting nurses, psychiatric evaluators, and community workers.
>
> The best protection employers can offer is to establish a zero-tolerance policy toward workplace violence against or by their employees. The employer should establish a workplace violence pre-vention program or incorporate the information into an existing acci-dent prevention program, employee handbook, or manual of standard operating procedures. It is critical to ensure that all employees know the policy and understand that all claims of workplace violence will be investigated and remedied promptly. In addition, employers can offer additional protections, such as the following:
>
>> Provide safety education for employees so they know what conduct is not acceptable, what to do if they witness or are subjected to workplace violence, and how to protect themselves. . . .
>
> The Occupational Safety and Health Act's (OSH Act) General Duty Clause requires employers to provide a safe and healthful work-place for all workers covered by the OSH Act. Employers who do not take reasonable steps to prevent or abate a recognized violence hazard in the workplace can be cited. Failure to implement suggestions in this fact sheet, however, is not in itself a violation of the General Duty Clause. . . .

OSHA has various publications, standards, technical assistance, and compliance tools to help you, and offers extensive assistance through its many safety and health programs: workplace consultation, voluntary protection programs, grants, strategic partnerships, state plans, training, and education. Guidance such as OSHA's Safety and Health Management Program Guidelines identify elements that are critical to the development of a successful safety and health management system. This and other information are available on OSHA's Web site at www.osha.gov.

Source: U.S. Department of Labor, Occupational Safety and Health Administration, OSHA Fact Sheet, "Workplace Violence," 2002

Operations

Risk assessment activities focus on tracking what pieces of the operation have the potential to incur loss or have incurred loss in the past. Record-keeping and inspection are common risk issues in this area. Other common risk areas include safety issues in the workplace. Compliance with legislation, including the Americans with Disabilities Act, is particularly important in terms of building design, serving clients, and accommodating employees with disabilities. Failure to comply with this legislation raises the possibility of sanctions that could have negative repercussions for the nonprofit organization.

Tracking the categories of comments and/or complaints identified by clients is essential in ensuring that the organization's clientele are receiving services in a manner that is understandable and of value. The manner in which services and procedures are explained to clients is an integral part of establishing a constructive dialogue and preventing potential claims of discrimination and/or differential treatment. The source of client complaints or criticism could be a misunderstanding of eligibility requirements or limitations on the types of service offered. All staff members should be thoroughly trained to serve clients, and training should be augmented by regularly scheduled in-service sessions that update the staff by discussing problems or conditions and offering the opportunity to make suggestions on better service for the clients.

Financial management is another area of potential risk in nonprofit operations. Financial discrepancies and mismanagement can result in legal problems, the erosion of the organization's donor base, and the creation of a difficult public relations situation. The thoroughness of written procedures is particularly important in the area of nonprofit finances because of the organization's tax-exempt status and sometimes fragile public trust.

Relations with the Public

Although preserving the nonprofit's tax exempt status is important, maintaining the public trust is equally important. The inherent damage caused by adverse publicity has the potential to devastate your nonprofit. Common risk areas include the mishandling of crisis situations and lack of skill in dealing with the media.

The nonprofit's good name and reputation can be damaged if it does not handle complaints, such as those from neighbors, effectively. Equally damaging can be the actions or misbehavior of staff and/or volunteers in a public setting. Common risk issues relate to the nonprofit's ability to supervise volunteers closely, particularly when they interact with the public.

IMPLEMENTATION OF RISK MANAGEMENT ACTIVITIES

Risk management activities are the action steps taken to treat identified risks. Here the nonprofit decides on the risk treatment options and determines what specific actions should be taken to reduce the potential or severity of the risks.

How Do You Deal with Risks Once You Identify Them?

Once you have identified and prioritized risks, you will need to determine a strategy to deal with them. As mentioned earlier, there are four primary methods of treating risks. Some are more appealing and practical than others, but in risk management, using these techniques is not an either/or proposition. Some effective risk management strategies combine two or more of these basic methods.

- *Avoidance.* Just say "no" and stop whatever it is that you are doing. This strategy usually is not an option in nonprofit operations. However, there may be some problematic aspect of the situation that can be eradicated. For example, if a program involves a process or activity that seems to cause problems, damage, or injury, your nonprofit might opt to redesign the program to eliminate that element.

- *Modification.* This is the most common risk management treatment. Modification means that the nonprofit changes policies, procedures, or the way in which certain things are done. Once a procedure is modified, the potential for loss from the risk is reduced because steps were taken to change the dynamics of the situation. For example, if there have been problems related to the way in which travel claims are reimbursed, the nonprofit can institute procedures and policies to standardize how travel claims paid.

- *Retention.* In this method of managing risk, the nonprofit sets up a special fund to pay for losses or increases the amount of the deductible on an insurance policy. An example would be raising the deductible for the nonprofit's auto policy so that claims under $1,000 would be paid by the nonprofit.

- *Transfer.* Risk can be transferred via purchase of insurance or by other contractual means. An example is the purchase of a comprehensive general liability policy (CGL) for the nonprofit.

Your nonprofit can choose one method or combine several to deal with identified risks. For example, your nonprofit might identify a risk area as insufficient internal controls in handling reimbursements. You could consider treating this risk by outsourcing the handling of the reimbursements to the vendor who does the nonprofit's payroll. This response can be considered an example of both avoidance and risk transfer: avoidance, as the activity is no longer done within the nonprofit; risk transfer, as the liability for handling this financial operation goes to the vendor. The risk could also be modified by implementing new policies and procedures for reimbursement of expenses.

Monitoring for Results: Did the Strategies Work?

The monitoring step ensures that the actions taken in the risk management implementation stage are reviewed to determine their effectiveness as well as to establish a framework for the next round of risk assessment. The strategies chosen to deal with identified risks might work as anticipated, or they might not. Unintended consequences are always a possibility. However, if a strategy does not work as expected, just chalk it up to experience and try something else.

There are numerous ways to evaluate the success of the risk management strategies that were applied to specific risks. Risk management techniques can be evaluated by:

- *Number of accidents.* Have the number of accidents decreased? Documentation is always important, but even more so once a risk management program is in place.

- *Documentation and analysis of accidents.* It is important to document not only accidents but also near misses. There may be a pattern that had not yet come to light.

- *Number of insurance claims and frequency and severity of losses.* Insurance claims are filed because a loss occurred that was covered by the policy. All insurance claims need to be documented. Your insurance professional can provide copies of claims if your files need to be updated. Once the risk management plan is in place, your nonprofit will want to track the number of claims that are filed to determine if the number of claims has decreased and by what percent.

- *Number of staff and volunteer complaints.* If the nonprofit's risk management strategies have addressed hot-button issue(s) in terms of staff and volunteer morale, it is important to track the number of complaints that come in after the risk treatment has been executed.

- *Internal controls.* Have policies and procedures been put in place *and enforced*? One of the most substantial areas for change is in the nonprofit's internal controls and the implementation of policies and procedures. An important outcome of risk management activities is the strengthening of the nonprofit's internal controls and infrastructure. New policies and procedures can be successful only if they are enforced. Changes in staff and management behavior and the types of behavior that the nonprofit rewards expectations are key elements in introducing effective risk management.

Risk Management as an Ongoing Process

Your nonprofit's risk management planning will not take hold unless *everyone* in the nonprofit understands what risk management is, how it works, and what their role is in effective risk management. Educational tools, such as slide presentations (via PowerPoint or other software), can be useful, especially if these are presented at in-service sessions. The information can be immediately available as a resource for staff and volunteers on the nonprofit's intranet or as an e-mail attachment.

As with any important change in your nonprofit, the concepts and practices associated with risk management are important for staff and volunteers to understand. Happily, risk management isn't rocket science. The concepts, principles, and practices are intuitive and easily understood. What may be harder for staff and volunteers to integrate is their role and new accountability for risk management behaviors. The educational materials your nonprofit presents must contain plenty of examples of how risk management activities would work in your nonprofit and clear descriptions of what is expected of staff and volunteers. New behaviors need to be illustrated—and modeled—by senior staff and board members.

Scheduling the Next Round of Risk Management Activities

The most important thing your team can do to ensure that your risk management planning will not simply sit on the shelf is to schedule the next round of risk management planning immediately. At the conclusion of your first DIAD session, schedule the next round for a date and time in three to six months. This time frame will give your team enough time to launch the training program for staff and volunteers and complete the deliverables that will emerge from the DIAD session.

SUMMARY

As your nonprofit begins its risk management planning, it is important to understand its value to the organization. It is just as important to understand why certain types of activities that have been traditionally billed as risk management do not produce quality results. Genuine risk management permeates the entire organization, enriches every activity, and promotes the long-term viability of your nonprofit.

CHAPTER 3

Using the Risk
Management Template

A small nonprofit called in a consultant to help them with risk management planning. The client appeared nervous and distracted. Having worked with this woman before, the consultant knew that that was not her usual demeanor. The consultant asked if anything was troubling her, and the client replied that the thought of assembling an entire risk management plan was daunting. The consultant assured her that the first round of planning involved using a template. As the client looked at the template, she exclaimed, "Fill in the blanks!! I love it—this is going to *work!*"

In Chapter 2 we examined the essential components of an effective risk management plan. Even if nonprofit managers and staff understand how risk management works, they may still feel overwhelmed by the task of putting it all together. There's no need to be concerned. The template we discuss in this chapter can facilitate the construction of the first draft of a risk management plan.

This useful tool helps your nonprofit quickly organize risk management activities by grouping the organization's main components. The template is a streamlined mechanism for assessing risk and achieving a concise risk management evaluation (see Exhibit 3.1). By using the template, you can identify risks and then prioritize to ensure a manageable agenda for risk management implementation. The template recognizes resource constraints in terms of time, staff, and money. *However, it is very*

EXHIBIT 3.1   TABLE OF CONTENTS: RISK MANAGEMENT PLAN FOR YOUR NONPROFIT

Goals and Objectives (brief overarching goal and short-term objectives)

- Overarching Goal—The Value Proposition of the Plan
- Short-term objectives of the Plan

The Nonprofit's Profile

- Address and contact information
- Number of years in operation
- Mission
- Names of board members and senior executives

Risk Assessment Section

Consider what risks may be present in these parts of the organization:

- Board
- Staffing/Volunteers
- Operations
- Relations with the Public

Prioritize the risks that were identified

- First priority risks—risks that will be addressed in this round of risk management planning
- Second priority risks—risk that will be addressed in the next round of risk management planning

Selecting a Strategy for Dealing with the Risks

First Priority Risks

For each risk, describe:

- Strategy for treating the risk. (Remember, the four choices are avoidance, retention, modification and transfer. You can combine parts of these treatments if necessary.)
- Desired outcomes/measures of success
- Resources needed to address these risks
- Responsibilities and timelines: who is responsible for doing what by a specific deadline
- Documentation of prior claims, occurrences (if applicable)

Simple metrics—Decide what the measures of success would be in treating each of these risks. For example, the metrics could include a reduction in the number of insurance claims or workplace accidents.

EXHIBIT 3.1   *CONTINUED*

Second Priority Risks

- List the risks that will be addressed in the next round of risk management planning

Summary of the Risk Management Plan

- Summary of risks selected for this round of risk management plan that includes the risk treatments selected, measures of success to be evaluated for each risk treatment, deliverables, deadlines, and name of individual responsible for the deliverables.
- Summary of training needs and policies to be reviewed.
- Review of previous risk management plan (if applicable) for the purposes of evaluating the success of the risk treatments.

Timetable for the next round of risk assessment and risk treatment

---

important to understand that the template is not intended to provide insurance or legal advice; readers are advised to consult with their insurance and/or legal advisors for specific assistance.

BUILDING A RISK MANAGEMENT PLAN

Goals and Objectives

This section presents a *brief* description of the plan's overarching goal and short-term objectives. The emphasis on brevity is to avoid the paralysis by analysis trap that many nonprofits experience in any kind of planning.

- *Value proposition of the plan (overarching goal).* Your nonprofit's primary goal in implementing a risk management plan may be the overall upgrade in the professionalism of the nonprofit's operations. Another example of an overarching goal is the strengthening of the nonprofit's internal controls and an improvement in systems management. There's no right or wrong answer—just keep your goal brief and relevant.

- *Short-term objectives of the projects.* (Note: You can add long-term objectives here if they are important to your nonprofit). For example, a good short-term objective might be to use the plan to reduce workplace injuries by 15 percent. Another example would be to integrate risk management practices throughout the non-profit's operations.

Here you briefly describe what your nonprofit would like to achieve and/or improve by implementing risk management planning. Perhaps your nonprofit has had some negative loss experience and the plan is a means of demonstrating your commitment to improving procedures and protocols. It's important to look at the big picture rather than get mired in the details. To simplify the process, consider these questions:

- What would you like the risk management plan to achieve in the next:
  - 3 months
  - 6 months
  - 1 year
  - Possibly change the way staff go about tasks related to their jobs?
  - Possibly change the way the nonprofit interacts with the community?
  - As a way of tracking insurance claims, accidents, and anything that would cause a loss or damage the nonprofit's reputation?

The objectives will help your team to see the big picture in terms of risk management planning and will facilitate their addressing risk areas that are consistent with the objectives.

The Nonprofit's Profile

This section of the template presents basic information about the organization, including address and contact information, years in operation, mission, names of board members and senior executives, and other information that would provide the reader with a thumbnail sketch of your nonprofit.

Risk Assessment

This section of the template presents the risks that will be addressed in this round of risk management planning. Users should identify the top risk areas for each of the nonprofit's organizational areas. As we discussed earlier, every nonprofit has these components, although they may be called by different titles.

Look at the real and potential problems that emerge from the four organizational components. Organize this section of the plan by listing the risks associated with board, staff, operations, and relations with the public. Consider the common problems that follow for each of the four organizational components.

Board

The board is the entity that is entrusted with the governance of the nonprofit. The focus of the risk assessment questions center on defining written standards for behavior and procedures within the board setting. Often the absence of written standards for behavior and procedures leads to practices that could incur liability for the board as a governance entity. The board's fiduciary obligations require very careful oversight of financial operations, including the nonprofit's annual audit and/or financial review.

The board is ultimately responsible for compliance with Sarbanes-Oxley legislation and any applicable state laws, such as California's Nonprofit Integrity Act. The board is expected to ensure that Sarbanes-Oxley requirements are being met by staff members and that best practices are being incorporated into the nonprofit's operations.

These questions address common problem areas.

- Does the board have a conflict of interest policy? Are board members required to sign a letter identifying any real or perceived conflicts of interest on an annual basis? This policy doesn't prevent a person with a real or potential conflict of interest from participating on a board, but it does document the conflict and establishes guidelines for dealing with real and potential conflicts in a commonsense way.

- Does an audit committee serve as the liaison between the auditor (or financial reviewer) and the board?

- Do board members have term limits? Have board members have been in place for over five years?

- Are family members and spouses seated on the board?

- Do board members attend meetings regularly? Is there a rule that requires board members to attend board meetings?

- Do the board meetings have agendas and minutes? Are the minutes prepared in a professional manner? Could an outside observer know, from the minutes, who was present, who was absent, what motions were voted on and the results?

- Does the board have directors' and officers' liability insurance?

- Are new board members required to attend a board orientation?

- Are board members briefed on new legislative developments, such as Sarbanes-Oxley legislation and any relevant state legislation?

Staff and Volunteers

Human resource management risk areas include such problems as harassment claims, workers' compensation costs, and wrongful termination. The areas of supervision, job description, and performance reviews have the potential to incur liability if they are not administered in a manner that can be demonstrated as competent. Background checks, as of motor vehicle or criminal records, must be addressed carefully for the protection of the nonprofit, its clients, and staff.

Many nonprofits are reluctant to supervise and discipline volunteers. This aversion appears to stem from the misguided belief that volunteers are just good-hearted individuals who offer their time to the nonprofit and are exempt from the accountability and performance expectations of employees. Nothing could be further from the truth! Volunteers are simply unpaid staff. The only discussion your nonprofit should not have with volunteers is about compensation packages and pensions. It is essential that volunteers be held to the same level of accountability as paid staff are. Nonprofits must enforce policies and procedures with both volunteer and paid staff. Both types of staff should also have avenues to address grievances and report unsafe conditions.

The next questions address common problem areas:

- Does the nonprofit have a whistleblower protection policy to protect staff and volunteers who report waste, fraud, or abuse?

- Are hiring and termination practices documented in an employee manual?

- Are the nonprofit's hiring and accommodation practices compliant with Americans with Disabilities (ADA) legislation?

- Has the nonprofit received complaints about supervisory practices? Are volunteers supervised in a manner consistent with supervisory practices of staff?

- Are there protocols for progressive discipline/termination of staff and volunteers?

- Does the nonprofit have grievance procedures (for issues other than waste, fraud, and abuse)?

- Do staff and volunteers have job descriptions, and do they receive performance evaluations on a regular basis?

- Does the nonprofit have written policies about sick leave, vacation, or other paid or unpaid time off?

- Does the nonprofit have written policies prohibiting inappropriate behavior, such as sexual harassment or drug/alcohol abuse? Do staff and volunteers have a confidential means of reporting these incidents? Does the nonprofit have a commitment to the staff to investigate such reports promptly and in a neutral manner?

Operations

The term "operations" describes what programs the nonprofit offers, how the nonprofit's office functions, and any other types of activities associated with the functioning of the organization. Some common areas of operation include:

- Finance
- Administration
- Programs
- Information technology
- Fundraising and advancement

The next questions address common problem areas:

- Does the nonprofit have written guidelines for payment of travel claims? For reimbursement of expenses? Are these guidelines enforced? Are senior management or board members permitted to evade these guidelines?

- Does the nonprofit have a document preservation policy that enables documents to be stored/archived in a user-friendly fashion? Does the nonprofit have a policy that prohibits the destruction of documents during an investigation or inquiry by regulators?

- Does the nonprofit produce reports, proposals, or other materials by specified deadlines?

- Does the nonprofit have eligibility requirements? If so, are the requirements clear and easy to understand? Can prospective clients easily obtain information on the nonprofit's programs?

- Are these internal controls in place:
  - Documentation for expenses (receipts, invoices, etc.) is required before reimbursement checks are issued.
  - Bank statements are forwarded (unopened) to the chief financial officer (CFO) or Executive Director (ED) for review.
  - The bookkeeper and/or other staff members who handle money are required to take at least one full week of vacation every year.
  - The organization has at least two signatories to sign checks.
  - No checks or money orders can be issued to the individual who signed the check. Another person must sign the check.
  - Bank deposits must be "for deposit only." No cash may be returned unless authorized by the ED, CFO, or member of the board's executive committee.
  - Financial reports must be prepared for board review on a monthly basis.
  - All check requests must be authorized by a senior manager other than the primary check signatory.
  - There must be an annual audit or financial review of the nonprofit's books. Auditors' recommendations must be implemented and compliance documented.

Relations with the Public

The nonprofit's good name and public trust can be damaged—perhaps permanently—through adverse publicity, the mishandling of a crisis, the personal appearance of staff and/or volunteers, the way in which staff and volunteers behave, the use of donor funds, or the way in which programs are administered.

These questions address common problem areas:

- Have there been incidents that potentially compromised the nonprofit's good reputation?
  - Did the incident involve staff or volunteer behavior toward a client, a donor, or the public?
  - Did the incident involve fundraising or a special event?
  - What were the key factors involved? How might the nonprofit modify its procedures to reduce the potential for another incident?
- Does the nonprofit have an effective public and media relations plan?
- Does the nonprofit handle complaints from neighbors effectively?
- Are there procedures to handle public comment and complaints?
- Does the nonprofit have vehicles with the organization's name on them? How are staff and volunteers screened and trained to drive?
- Do staff and volunteers understand that their deportment and personal appearance reflect on the public image of the nonprofit?
  - How are staff and volunteers monitored and supervised to ensure that the nonprofit's positive public image is maintained?

Prioritize the Risks

Compile a list of the risk areas that your nonprofit wants to address in this round of risk management planning. Particularly for the first round of risk management planning, it is important to select a workable number of risks—those risk areas that are of paramount concern at the present time. You can address other, less vital risks in subsequent planning sessions.

Selecting a Strategy for Dealing with the Risks

This section of the template describes how each of the risks (from the previous section) will be treated.

For *each* risk, describe:

- Strategy for treating the risk. (Remember, you can use more than one risk treatment.)
- Desired outcomes/measures of success
- Resources needed to address these risks
- Responsibilities and timelines: who is responsible for doing what by a specific deadline
- Documentation of prior claims, occurrences (if applicable)

Repeat the process of selecting a strategy to deal with each risk listed in the Risk Assessment section. This is why it is important to choose a *workable* number of risks for your first risk management planning session. As your team gains experience, other staff members can be transitioned in and the process refined to fit your nonprofit's needs.

Summarize by creating a table that shows the risks that will be addressed this year; what will be done; when it will be done; and who is responsible for the action.

Second-Priority Risks

List the risks that will be addressed in the next round of risk assessment (which will take place in three months, six months, or a year).

The next step is deciding how your nonprofit wants to deal with each of the risks on the list. To review, the four basic risk treatment methods:

1. *Avoidance.* To avoid risk, you just say "no" and stop whatever it is that you are doing. This is usually not an option in nonprofit operations. However, you may able to eradicate some problematic aspect of the situation.

2. *Retention.* In retaining risk, the nonprofit sets up a special fund to pay for losses or increases the amount of the deductible on an insurance policy.

3. *Modification.* In modification, you change policies, procedures, or the way in which certain things are done. This is the most common method of risk management treatment. Through modification, you reduce the potential for loss from the risk because you take steps to change the dynamics of the situation.

4. *Transfer.* You can transfer risk via purchase of insurance or by other contractual means.

An easy way to *organize* the strategy is to:

- *Identify the primary method(s) for addressing the risk.* Remember, you can utilize more than one risk treatment method. Perhaps the risk needs to be addressed by changing how something is done, adding safety procedures, or increasing the deductible on the relevant insurance policy.

- *List the desired outcomes/measurements of success.* The strategy for dealing with a particular risk should include a brief comment on the desired outcome and what would indicate that the strategy was successful. In other words, what does success look like? You'll need this information in three to six months when you look back on the risk strategy to see if it needs to be fine-tuned.

- *Document prior claims, occurrences (if applicable).* If possible, include reference to documentation of prior claims or occurrences as a baseline. During the evaluation component, you can compare the results of the risk treatment to this baseline.

- *List resources needed to address this risk.* Does the risk treatment need to include safety equipment, training, and evaluation of ergonomics? If so, you must identify the necessary resources.

When you have compiled a risk treatment strategy for each risk, you can compile this information into a chart like the one shown in Exhibit 3.2.

Action Steps for Risk Treatment

The next step is to assign action items for each risk and, more important, to identify deliverables and assign responsibility and deadlines. You

EXHIBIT 3.2   SAMPLE SUMMARY OF RISK TREATMENT STRATEGIES AND ASSIGNMENTS

Risks	Strategy	Person Assigned
No Whistleblower Protection Policy.	Draft a whistleblower protection policy and a process for making reports of waste, fraud, and abuse.	Susan Smith
Stairway to second floor needs repair.	Repair stairs at the top of the stairway.	Bob Jones
Nonprofit's vans have been involved in 5 accidents this year.	Review accident reports to determine if cause of accidents is mechanical or driver error. Institute a routine maintenance process for all vehicles. Require all drivers to complete a safety training to be held at the nonprofit.	Fred Green and Mary Mayfield

will not be able to treat the risks for this round of planning in a coherent manner unless you assign specific deliverables along with individual responsibility and deadlines. These measures will begin to pave the way for future rounds of risk management planning. The idea is to institute risk management as a repetitive cycle of planning. This cycle cannot take hold unless you specify both *action* and *results*.

The sum total of the action steps becomes the risk management plan for the current round of risk management planning. Review all of the deliverables in terms of the objectives of the risk management planning: Are the risk areas selected consistent with the risk management planning objectives? Do they represent a new objective that needs to be articulated?

The risk areas that were not chosen for action in the current round become the first risk areas studied in the next round of risk assessment. These risk areas may or may become the priority risk areas for the next round, depending on circumstances at that time.

Simple Metrics to Monitor the Results

This section of the template describes what the nonprofit expects to achieve in dealing with the risks listed in the last section. You should clearly state the measures of success in treating the first-round risks as well as expected results for specific risk treatments.

For example, if the risk area identified is the number of accidents in vehicles owned by the nonprofit, risk treatments could include additional training and supervision of drivers (modification) and increasing the deductible for the auto policy (retention). The measure of success could be gauged at a reduction of the number of auto accidents by 35 percent in the next six months. The action items would include raising the insurance deductible to $1,000, presenting additional driver training sessions, and developing more stringent policies to supervise drivers. The deliverables would be the curriculum for the training and the written policy on supervision of drivers. These action items and deliverables would be consistent with one of the nonprofit's overall objectives in risk management planning: the reduction of insurance claims and accidents.

Timetable for the Next Round of Risk Management Activities

This section outlines the timeline for the next round of risk management planning. Every current risk management plan should have a concluding section that sets a timeline for reviewing the current risk management activities and beginning a new round of risk assessment. For the first two years, your nonprofit should plan on having at least two to three rounds of risk management activities every year.

SUMMARY

Using a risk management template can help to facilitate and streamline risk management planning. The structure of the template lends itself to apportioning tasks and leveraging the productivity of smaller work groups, particularly in preparation activities for the Done in a Day session.

CHAPTER 4

Done in a Day Session for Risk Management

HOW TO PREPARE FOR THE DIAD SESSION

Success in any Done in a Day (DIAD) planning is contingent on the quality of preparation. The more complete the preparation, the faster the progress in assembling the first edition of a plan. The suggestions that follow can help you save time, energy, and money.

- *Assemble a risk management team.* Select high-quality people to be on the team who are very knowledgeable about one or more of the nonprofit's organizational components. It is particularly important to assemble a team of the nonprofit's star "players" for the first round of risk management planning. Ensure that the team has sufficient resources to produce a quality plan, even if that means shifting workloads or delaying delivery of projects. The team should also receive small perks for their work on this project. The perk need not be elaborate or expensive but should be something that the individual team member would enjoy—perhaps a gift card to a coffee shop or one week's reserved parking in a prime location or even a prepaid ticket for public transportation in your area (e.g., a $10 rail pass).

- *Assemble only that information which is necessary and sufficient.* One of the biggest challenges that nonprofits face in assembling their first risk management plan is "data dump"—staff members believe that more is better in terms of the volume of information that is brought to the plan. Emphasize that material is not useful unless it is relevant.

- *Be aware of hidden and not so hidden barriers.* Resolve to push through them. Some examples of barriers that are subtle yet potent enough to derail planning include the excuse that not all of the committee members are available on the date chosen for the DIAD session. Insist on mandatory attendance, and arrange for other obligations to be handled by a substitute. The team members need to be fully on board with the planning. Ensure that this planning has the full and visible endorsement of the board and senior management. Be prepared for the possibility that a member of the team will be ill on the day of the planning. Make sure that the team includes individuals who can fill in for someone who is ill or unavailable at the last minute. *The better prepared you are, the better the quality of planning for the DIAD session.* Discuss the information that will need to be included in the risk management plan and assign the team members to prepare those materials.

- *Consider how the risk management plan template can be used to educate the organization's board, staff, and volunteers.* To implement an effective risk management plan, you must train the DIAD team and the nonprofit's board, staff, and volunteers. You can simplify training by following the template.

- *Consider asking your insurance professional, financial professional, information technology professional, and/or legal professional to sit in on at least part of the DIAD session for feedback and input.* The nonprofit's professional advisors are excellent sources of guidance in the design and content of your risk management plan. These individuals may not be available for the entire DIAD session but probably would be willing to sit in on part of the session or review the plan that was assembled from the session. These professionals know your nonprofit's needs, intricacies, and challenges. They can also help you to leverage your risk management plan for additional benefits. Chapter 9 reviews the types of benefits that can be reaped from an effective plan.

Timetable for Preparation

The timeline that follows is a sample of how long a nonprofit needs to prepare adequately for a DIAD session. Your nonprofit may need less time. In generally, it is sufficient to begin gathering the types of material needed for a first round of planning three weeks prior to the DIAD session. Always remember that you will schedule another round of planning at the conclusion of each DIAD session.

The risk areas that you chose to include in the first round of risk management planning should be significant, but they are by no means all-inclusive.

Three Weeks in Advance

- Choose the date and book the room. Work to ensure that, as many key players are available that day, but *choose a date and stick to it!* It is particularly important to have a backup person who fully participates in the prep and the planning for each key player. (Such backups will be needed for the business continuity plan anyway.)

- Identify the staff and/or volunteers, including board members, who should be seated on the first risk management committee. These individuals need not be senior management, but all need to be highly competent self-starters. Everyone on the team will be a "backup" to another member. The individuals should be advised that they are *required* to attend the DIAD session and to *participate fully* in the brief preparatory work. Team members also need to know that on the day of the DIAD session, they will not have access to cell phones and pagers. They need to advise family that emergency phone calls must go to the receptionist (or person designated as such that day).

- Engage a facilitator for the session. The individual should be knowledgeable about organizational behavior and, if possible, about risk management or insurance. The individual can be a senior executive or member of the board or an outside consultant. The facilitator should be given a copy of the template, worksheets, and any other documents that you will want to use to construct the first edition of the risk management plan. The facilitator should understand that the DIAD session is the launch of an ongoing risk management planning program. As part of the DIAD session, the dates of upcoming rounds of risk assessment, risk management strategies, and evaluation should be selected.

Two Weeks in Advance

- Present the documentation of support from the board and senior management. Briefly describe to a selected group (the risk management team) the need to begin a cycle of risk management planning, and explain that the DIAD session will include an educational piece on risk management planning and best practices. For now, the team will look at the areas of the nonprofit that have been troublesome in the past or are in need of upgrade.

  The team will divide the risk assessment task into several small groups and center on a specific function area: board, staff/volunteers, operations, or relations with the public. The group should meet once or twice (at most) and should list what they see as problem areas or issues in the part of the organization they are assigned to review. The task should be framed to identify issues in this way:
  - Are there any accidents, insurance claims, complaints, or other important incidents that are documented?
  - Is there a history of incidents that may or may not be documented?
  - What are the problem areas in this function?
  - What are the current internal controls that relate to this function? Are there any problems?
  - How does the information technology related to this function work? Is it secure? Does this function handle sensitive material? How is that kept safe?

Deliverables for each function group include:

- Selection of a leader/backup
- A list of those issues identified in their functional area with recommendations for which have higher priority

- Documents or excerpts, if there are any, to support their prioritization of the issues

One Week in Advance

- Confirm that the work groups are on track, but *DON'T CHANGE THE DIAD DATE* if they are not on track. Anything that is missing will be added to the day's agenda, and the session will be a bit longer. Make it clear that their deliverables are due in time for the DIAD session.
- Remind team members that they need to give family members the phone number of the receptionist on duty that day as cell phones and pagers will be banned from the session.
- Brief the facilitator on the progress so far and how the agenda for the session will be structured. Be sure to review the deliverables for the day and the session timeline to ensure that a beginning, middle, and an end are scheduled.

The Week of the Session

- Have a "walk-through" meeting for the team and the facilitator at least three days prior to the session to review the agenda and to ensure that the checklist for materials is complete, that there are backups for the team members, and that there are backups for the people who are tasked with bringing materials and refreshments.
- Order food and beverages for lunch and breaks.
- Brief reception staff on taking messages for the team members.
- Schedule supplies and materials to be in place in the meeting room on the day of the session. Materials needed include:
    - Flip chart with markers.
    - Laptop computer (used for the slide presentation and to record the findings for the first edition of the risk management plan) and printer.

        Important! Designate a "recording secretary" for the session. This individual need not be a member of the team, but could be a clerical staff member or key volunteer. The individual should be conversant with the use of a laptop and with word processing software.

- LCD projector.
- Coffee, water, and/or other refreshments for team members.
- "Perks" to be distributed at the end of the sessions.

As the preparation for the session commences, the team leader should document what is needed for the session, where supplies and refreshments were obtained, and any other information that can be saved to facilitate the setup of the next round of risk management planning.

THE DIAD SESSION

You will assemble the first edition of your risk management plan during this Done in a Day session. This section will guide your nonprofit on the development of a *timed* agenda and recommendations for recommendations for keeping the discussion moving and ensuring that the planning keeps moving forward.

Before the session begins, ensure that the team members are completely focused on the session. Cell phones and pagers must be *turned off. Team members may not take phone calls or return to their desks at any time during the DIAD session.* Emergency phone calls are to be routed to a designated receptionist. Make sure there are alternates on the team in case someone is absent or called away for an emergency. The session should continue despite an absent member.

The facilitator and the team leadership need to be committed to keeping the discussion moving along. The facilitator should advise the team members that she or he has the prerogative to intervene to redirect the conversation when a participant is either attempting to dominate or is long-winded. Keeping track of the time for each of the sections is vital to the success of the day. The times listed for each section are for illustration purposes only. You may assign any length of time to each segment. Keep in mind that the longer a session goes, the more likely fatigue will impair planning progress.

Sample Agenda

DIAD Session Agenda

[Estimated Time = 6 hours 45 minutes including breaks and lunch]

Part I   Introduction to Risk Management and Review of Agenda
[40 minutes]

Part II   Risk Assessment Review and Selection [60 minutes]

Break [15 minutes] Team members may not return to their desks
during the break.

Part II   Risk Assessment Review and Selection Continued
[20 minutes]

Part III   Risk Management Strategies: Choosing a Method to
Address Each Risk [90 minutes]

Lunch   [45 minutes] Lunch is served in the meeting room. Team
members may not return to their desks during lunch.

Part IV   Strategies for Organizational Change [60 minutes]

Break [15 minutes] Team members may not return to their desks
during the break.

Part V   Preparing to Present the Risk Management Plan to the
Board [40 Minutes]

Part VI   Next Steps [20 minutes]

Sample Format of a DIAD Session

A sample "script" of a presentation that the facilitator and/or team
leader can use to preside over the DIAD session follows.

Part I How to Conduct the DIAD Session [40 minutes]

This educational piece is the "executive summary" of the more extensive training for staff and volunteers that is presented in Chapter 8. The
intent is to review the basic steps in risk management planning and
describe how the session will be structured.

Here is a sample outline that can be incorporated into a slide presentation. It is often useful to structure Part 1 as a slide presentation. The
box outlines the format of such a presentation.

Introduction to Risk Management Planning
Training Curriculum Outline

What Is Risk Management?

Risk management is the means by which nonprofits can identify, assess, and control risks that may be present within their organizational structure or operations.

Three key activities in risk management are:
1. Risk assessment
3. Implementation of risk management activities
4. Monitoring for results

What Is Risk Assessment?
- Risk assessment is the process of evaluating potential for accidents, injuries, insurance claims, or adverse publicity.
- Risks areas are prioritized, and possible risk treatment approaches are considered.

What Are Risk Management Activities?

Risk management activities are action steps that are taken once risk areas are identified. The people who are designing the risk management plan need to decide how they want to try to reduce the potential for the risk, or for the damage that the risk might cause. There are four basic methods for treating risk:

1. *Avoidance.* Just say "no" and stop whatever it is that you are doing. This is usually not an option in nonprofit operations. However, you may be able to eradicate some problematic aspect of the situation.
2. *Retention.* In retaining risk, the nonprofit sets up a special fund to pay for losses or increases the amount of the deductible on an insurance policy.
3. *Modification.* In modification, you change policies, procedures, or the way in which certain things are done. This is the most common method of risk management

treatment. Through modification, you reduce the potential for loss from the risk because you take steps to change the dynamics of the situation.

4. *Transfer.* You can transfer risk via purchase of insurance or by other contractual means.

What Is Monitoring for Results?

This step ensures that the actions taken in the risk management implementation stage are reviewed to determine their effectiveness and to establish a framework for the next round of risk assessment.

Benefits of Using a Risk Management Template

- The template is a streamlined mechanism for assessing risk and achieving a concise risk management evaluation.
- Risks are prioritized to ensure a manageable agenda for risk management implementation.
- The template is designed to recognize resource constraints in time, staff, and money.

What Are the Risks That Can Destroy Your Nonprofit?

- Financial mismanagement and noncompliance with Sarbanes-Oxley legislation
- Costly human resources litigation stemming from wrongful termination, sexual harassment, or workers' compensation claims
- Criminal activity by a member of the staff or a volunteer
- Loss of revenue from major client or funder or loss of a contract with the private or public sector
- Product liability claims
- Litigation or criminal investigation stemming from abuse of children or members of a vulnerable population
- Problems with the IRS—either penalties related to tax reporting or, for nonprofits, loss of 501(c)(3) designation

How Does a Nonprofit Assemble a Risk Management Plan?
There are five steps to risk management planning:

Step 1.   Assess Your Risk.

Here you determine what risks are present in the nonprofit and the potential severity of those risks.

Step 2.   Select a Risk Treatment.

Here you choose how you want to treat a particular risk. There are four primary ways to treat risk: avoidance, retention, modification, and transfer. A combination of two or more of these methods also can be used.

Step 3.   Identify Action Steps for Risk Treatment.

Once a decision is made in terms of risk treatment, then you identify action steps that include specific deliverables and deadlines and naming the individual who will take the lead on the action.

Step 4.   Establish Simple Metrics to Monitor the Results.

This step documents what "success" would look like for each of the risk treatment strategies. The metrics can be as simple as "reduce the frequency of accidents to no more than two a year."

Step 5.   Timetable for the Next Round of Risk Management Activities.

Risk management planning needs to become a routine event in the nonprofit's operations. Scheduling the next round of risk management planning establishes tighter deadlines for risk assessment and for monitoring the results of the previous round of risk management activities.

Summary and Q&A

Next Steps for the Facilitator

The facilitator continues the discussion by walking the team members through the template outline, as discussed in detail in Chapter 6.

The template is the logical extension of the slide presentation as it represents the basic framework for the risk management plan. Next, the facilitator presents the session deliverables, with emphasis on their documentation and the assignment of individual responsibility for deadlines.

Some examples of deliverables include:

- A risk management plan for at least X number of risk areas that identifies desired outcomes, deliverables, deadlines, and individuals responsible for the deliverables

- A plan to present training on risk management to the board, staff, and volunteers

- A timetable for the next round of risk management planning

Part II Risk Assessment Review and Selection
[60 minutes]

In this segment, each of the work groups will review its findings before the entire group. The facilitator should explain how this preliminary work provides the foundation for risk assessment activities. The discussion should be structured as follows:

- Each work group (board, staff and volunteers, operations, and relations with the public) should provide a list of its findings, including recommendations for priority risks (the risks that should be addressed in this round of risk management planning).

- The facilitator should list priority risks from each group on a flip chart and then open the discussion to prioritize the risks. The risks should be segmented into Tier 1 (top priority) and Tier 2. Tier 1 risks are those that the nonprofit should deal with in this round of risk management planning. Tier 2 risks represent issues that would be addressed in the next round of risk management activities (in three to six months). Remember, it is important to choose a workable number of risk areas. The next round of risk management planning can be scheduled for as soon as three months from today's session.

- The Tier 1 and Tier 2 lists should be transcribed onto the template (on the laptop). These factors should be considered when deciding on how many risks to address in this round:
  - An important factor in deciding which risks to treat in this round of risk assessment are those risk areas that are particularly troublesome either in terms of number of accidents/losses or those that would cause the nonprofit's insurance to be cancelled or renewed at a much higher premium. For example, the nonprofit has had a number of workers' compensation claims or if the nonprofit's van has been involved in a number of accidents. These risks would be given high priority because there is an immediate need to remedy the situation— particularly if the price and availability of insurance is at stake.
  - Another important consideration is dealing with those risk areas that are keeping the nonprofit out of compliance with federal, state, or local laws or regulations. For example, if the nonprofit does not have a whistleblower protection policy or a document preservation policy, it is not in compliance with Sarbanes-Oxley legislation.
  - Choosing which risks to deal with first sometimes depends on the size of the nonprofit and the number of staff members who can work on strategies for mitigation. The risks that leave the nonprofit vulnerable should be addressed first.
  - The nonprofit's insurance, legal, or financial professionals can help by pointing out risk areas that need attention. For example, if your auditor recommends that your nonprofit tighten its procedures around travel claims, then this recommendation should move immediately to a Tier 1 risk.

Break [15 minutes] Team members may *not* return to their desks during the break.

**Part II Risk Assessment Review and Selection
Continued [20 minutes]**
Summarize the discussion and review the selection of risks that will be addressed in this round of risk management planning.

Part III Risk Management Strategies: Choosing a Method to Address Each Risk [90 minutes]

For each of the risks chosen, decide on a risk treatment strategy that might combine two or more of the basic techniques. For example:

- The nonprofit has identified the inconsistent method by which travel claims are processed as a risk area. Risk treatment strategies might include implementing a policy that outlines what paperwork is required to document expenses for reimbursement. The policy could also require all staff members to obtain written permission from their supervisor before going on a business trip and limiting the amount that could be charged on a daily basis for meals and incidentals. Another risk treatment strategy could be a review of travel claims submitted within the past three to six months. Individuals who received excessive compensation might be required to refund the sum.

- The nonprofit has had numerous automobile accidents with the agency's van. Risk management strategies could include additional training for staff members and volunteers who drive the van, a supervisor observing the driving techniques of everyone who drives the van, a safety check of the van, and an increase in the deductible for the automobile insurance policy.

Every strategy to address individual risks must contain three essentials:

1. *The primary method(s) for addressing the risk.* Remember, more than one risk treatment method can be utilized. Perhaps the risk needs to be addressed by changing how something is done, adding safety procedures, and increasing the deductible on the relevant insurance policy.

2. *Desired outcomes/measurements of success.* The strategy for dealing with a particular risk should include a brief comment on the desired outcome and what would indicate that the strategy was successful. In other words, what does success look like? You'll need this information in about three to six months, when you look back on the risk strategy to see if it needs to be fine-tuned.

EXHIBIT 4.1   RISK MANAGEMENT PLAN:
SAMPLE ACTION SUMMARY

Risk	Deliverable	Deadline	Staff/Volunteer
Sidewalk uneven	Repave damaged section	May 3	Joe
Fundraising event needs risk assessment	Review event venue and program to identify and address risks	July 15	Team: Mary (leader) Frank, Bill, Susan and Charlotte
Vehicles in 3 minor accidents over the past 6 months	Reduce accidents by refresher training for all drivers	August 20	Amy

3. *Documentation of prior claims, occurrences (if applicable).* If possible, include references to documentation of prior claims or occurrences as a baseline. The results of the risk treatment can be compared to this baseline during the evaluation component.

Once a strategy is determined, establish a timeline for the deliverables, and identify who will take the lead and what resources will be necessary to bring about the deliverables. Do this for each of the risk areas, and complete the template page that captures this information. When you have compiled a risk treatment strategy for each risk, compile it into a chart like the one shown in Exhibit 4.1.

The facilitator should summarize the risks and risk strategies chosen for this round of risk management planning. The summary is the non-profit's first edition of its risk management plan. At the end of this segment, the team leader should transcribe the risk strategies onto the template file on the laptop.

Lunch [45 Minutes] Lunch is served in the meeting room. Team members may *not* return to their desks during this segment.

Part IV Strategies for Training: How to Introduce Lasting Organizational Change [60 minutes]

Review the action steps to mitigate each of the risks in this round of risk management planning. Consider the types of training and/or policies that need to be put in place or reviewed to reinforce the risk treatments. The team should also consider how to facilitate change in operations and organizational culture to further reinforce risk management practices. Set the dates/times to present risk management training to the staff and volunteers. These presentations should be completed within two weeks of the DIAD session.

Break [15 minutes] Team members may *not* return to their desks during the break.

Part V Preparing to Present the Risk Management Plan to the Board [40 Minutes]

Complete the transcription of the proceedings onto the template and backup the file. Electronic versions of the template will be distributed to the board and all staff after the meeting.

Outline a presentation on the risk management template findings to the board. Book the date of this presentation; it should take place within three weeks of the DIAD session.

Sample Outline: Presentation for the Board

- Introduction of the risk management team
- Executive Summary of generic risk management activities and structure of the template
- Presentation of the summary of risk areas chosen and corresponding risk treatment strategies.
- Presentation of training strategies
- Timeline for next round of risk management planning

The board presentation should also include an opportunity for board members to ask questions and make recommendations for expanding the scope of the risk management plan.

Part VI Next Steps [20 minutes]

The facilitator asks the team to set up dates for the next round of risk management planning. For the first two years, the rounds should take place every three to six months; thereafter, meetings can be held annually.

The team leader should thank the team and the facilitator for their hard work, distribute perks, and adjourn the session.

SUMMARY

The DIAD risk management session is the first step in launching a sustainable risk management program for your nonprofit. Preparation is key to success, as is having a facilitator and a team leader who can convey the vision and value proposition of this type of planning to the team and, ultimately, to the entire organization.

PART TWO

Business Continuity Planning

CHAPTER 5

Business Continuity Planning

TWO IMPORTANT LESSONS FROM SEPTEMBER 11

The tragedy of September 11 illustrated two important lessons about business continuity planning. Morgan Stanley was one of the companies that had offices in the World Trade Center. This company was well aware of the damage that a terrorist attack could produce. Terrorists bombed the World Trade Center in 1993, inflicting heavy damage on the Morgan Stanley offices. Company management understood that the terrorists were persistent and that it was not a case of "if" but "when" the next attack would take place. After the 1993 bombing, Morgan Stanley brought in a consultant to engage in monthly disaster drills. During these drills, everyone was to exit the building via the nearest emergency exit. These drills took place every month for the next eight years. When the alarm sounded on September 11, everyone in the Morgan Stanley offices evacuated the building and kept moving. Very few members of the Morgan Stanley staff lost their lives that morning.

Sarah Ferguson, Duchess of York, established the Chances for Children foundation that was headquartered in the World Trade Center. In an interview subsequent to September 11 attacks, CNN's Larry King asked the duchess how long she anticipated it would take for her foundation to resume operations and whether she was planning to reopen the offices in another location. The duchess replied, "Larry, the foundation is already up and running. We raised close to $100,000 for the 9/11 fund which we started . . ." (Transcript, *Larry King Live,* CNN, November 16, 2001)

The two important lessons from September 11 are:

1. Business interruptions are a part of the life of any organization and should be expected. Even though a business interruption is not usually the result of terrorist activities, any interruption can send the organization's operations into crisis mode.

2. Business interruptions, even ones as catastrophic as the events of September 11, need not destroy the nonprofit if a plan is in place to manage crisis incidents and resume business operations.

Morgan Stanley and Chances for Children, one a corporation and the other a nonprofit, planned for business interruptions and survived the horrific events of September 11. These two examples illustrate that business continuity planning can be just as effective for a nonprofit as it can be for a private sector firm.

WHAT IS BUSINESS CONTINUITY PLANNING?

It is 8:00 on a Saturday night. A fire has started on the seventh floor of the building housing the Hometown Social Services Agency (HSSA). By the time the firefighters arrive, the entire seventh floor is engulfed. Sprinklers throughout the building have been activated, and there is approximately three feet of standing water on each floor. The building has been red-tagged. Firefighters have determined that the flooring on the seventh floor has been seriously compromised, and in several places the floor has crashed into the HSSA offices below. When a building is "red-tagged" by the building inspector, no one is allowed to enter the building until it has been repaired. Wiring and telecommunications infrastructure have been seriously damaged. Building inspectors believe that the building will remain uninhabitable for at least six weeks.

If you were the executive director of the HSSA, what would you do? How would you ensure that your board knew what happened and that your staff knew what to do on Monday morning?

Business continuity planning is the means by which a company or a nonprofit can develop and document the policies, procedures, activities, and protocols necessary to resume essential business operations immediately following a business interruption. Business continuity planning is an important companion piece to risk management planning. A well-crafted risk management plan can facilitate the design of an effective business continuity plan; conversely, a well-crafted business continuity plan can be the foundation for the design of a risk management plan.

There are three primary components to a business continuity plan:

1. *Crisis Incident Management Component.* The initial crisis scenario needs to be addressed before the nonprofit can even consider the steps it needs to take to resume operation. In today's media-driven environment, a solid crisis communications strategy is essential to preserving your nonprofit's good name and providing quality information to support emergency fundraising. A section in this chapter is devoted to crafting a crisis communication plan for your nonprofit.

2. *Business Resumption Component.* Once the nonprofit has dealt with the immediate crisis, it needs to begin work immediately to resume operations. This stage of the plan needs to clearly describe the nonprofit's important functions and prioritize/sequence the functional areas that need to be in place to resume operations.

3. *Emergency Fundraising Component.* The emergency fundraising component often occurs in parallel with the crisis incident management and the business resumption components. It is treated here, however, as a distinct component because emergency fundraising is central to the rebuilding of the nonprofit or the acquisition of a new office location.

    Important: Emergency fundraising can generate its own crisis scenario if it not conducted in a professional and ethical manner.

Of the many cautionary tales of damage to a nonprofit's good name by mismanaging an emergency fundraising campaign, the story of the Red Cross's error of judgment in handling the Liberty Fund is instructive because this organization is routinely accused of mishandling disaster-related funds. Following the September 11 attacks on New York and Washington, the American Red Cross (ARC) launched a phenomenally successful fundraising drive. Monetary donations poured into the local chapters and headquarters. The Red Cross claimed that all of the monetary donations received in this campaign were going to be used to assist the surviving families of people who were killed in the attacks. The ARC president at the time, Dr. Bernadine Healy, established the Liberty Fund as the exclusive account for these donations. Historically, money collected by the ARC from disaster-related fundraising efforts was put into the overall budget for ARC Disaster Services. Prior to this disaster, fundraising materials never contained any written assurance to donors that *all* of the money collected for a specific disaster would be used exclusively for that purpose. Traditionally, the Red Cross Disaster Services division at their National Headquarters leveraged whatever the current "disaster" was as a means of raising money to support future disaster scenarios. Red Cross "insiders" were outraged that Dr. Healy chose to segregate the enormous sums being donated as a result of the September 11 attacks. As pressure began to mount to commingle the Liberty Fund donations with the rest of the disaster relief funds, Dr. Healy delayed the payment of gifts to the victims' families. The families complained to Congress, and soon Senator Charles Grassley (R–Iowa), chair of the Senate Finance Committee, began to investigate. The ARC subsequently changed its position, and stated that all of the Liberty Fund monies would be distributed to victims' families. Dr. Healy was forced to resign as ARC president shortly thereafter.

As your nonprofit begins to plan to deal with crises and business interruptions, it is important to consider the implications of its responses carefully. Maintaining public trust as your nonprofit emerges from a business interruption should always be a primary consideration.

SOURCES OF BUSINESS
INTERRUPTIONS

Your nonprofit's operations can be interrupted in any number of ways. The examples that follow illustrate some of the more common disruptions of normal business operations.

- *Fire—in your building or an adjacent office.* Even if a fire takes place in a neighboring office or building, your nonprofit's operations could be adversely affected. Smoke and water damage from a fire in an adjacent office can damage all of the other offices to the point that a building inspector declares the entire building off limits. Sprinkler systems are often triggered by heat or smoke and will automatically activate and sound an alarm at the same time. Depending on the system, the sprinklers may be divided into "zones" to minimize the damage, but if your office is in the zone where the sprinklers were activated, it could be affected even if the fire was not there. The closer your office is to the actual fire, the more likely it will sustain smoke and water damage.

- *Street closures due to civil unrest or infrastructure problems.* If the street(s) leading up to your nonprofit are closed due to an emergency, civil unrest, or damage to the street infrastructure, your staff, volunteers, and clients will be unable to access your offices.

- *Loss of electrical power.* Blackouts, brownouts, or failure of a regional power grid could plunge your nonprofit into darkness and possibly cause serious damage to your information technology structure.

- *Natural disasters, such as floods, earthquakes, hurricanes, or blizzards.* The indelible images of Hurricane Katrina should serve as a model for the type of devastation caused by a natural disaster. The controversies over the quality and timeliness of support from the public sector should also serve as a cautionary tale. It is unrealistic to assume that your nonprofit will be supported in its recovery by government at any level. A business continuity plan will facilitate greater self-sufficiency and could serve to help your nonprofit survive any natural disaster.

- *Corruption of financial or operational databases.* Nonprofits, like any other business, live and die by their computers, databases, software, and electronic files—not to mention personal digital assistants (PDAs), cell phones, and the like. The virulent "blaster" virus that was transmitted through the Internet caused the Maryland Department of Motor Vehicles to be closed for three days. Today's computer worms do not require opening up an e-mail. Merely activating your Internet browser can introduce dangerous worms and spyware.

- *Loss of major donor(s) or contracts.* Your nonprofit can be seriously damaged without any physical traces. The loss of funding from a contract, major donor, or other source of funding can have a serious, if not devastating, impact on your operations.

- *Loss of essential members of staff or executive team through sudden death or leaving the organization (under a cloud or not).* Key members of your staff can have specialized skills, institutional history/memory, contacts, and other attributes that add value to their place in the organization. When a key staff member leaves under any circumstances, the normal operation of the nonprofit is affected. If the key member dies or is in legal trouble, the impact of the loss can resonate throughout the entire organization.

- *Violence in the workplace.* Sadly, violence in the workplace, particularly as a spillover of domestic violence, is becoming more and more commonplace. Often these incidents cannot be anticipated, but they can have a chilling effect not only on the surviving staff and the nonprofit's operations, but also on the image of the organization.

- *Crime and criminal acts.* The theft of important materials or valuables can leave a nonprofit in a vulnerable position. Consider the implications for a West Coast arts organization whose computers and server were stolen. The server contained contact information for all of the organization's donors, including their credit card numbers, and no backup existed. The nonprofit went to the media to publicize the burglary. How do you think donors felt when they learned that their credit card information was compromised?

- *Adverse publicity.* As with the last example, any kind of adverse publicity can act as a distraction or obstacle to normal operations.

All of these examples point to the need to have a solid plan in place for dealing with the immediate crisis and then taking the necessary steps to resume full operations. The first step in dealing with a crisis in today's age of 24/7 media coverage is an effective crisis communication plan.

CRISIS COMMUNICATION PLAN

In today's media-driven world, any crisis scenario attracts media coverage almost immediately. If your nonprofit does not have a spokesperson who is skilled in media relations, your organization's public image could be adversely affected.

The following story illustrates how quickly a respected nonprofit can fall from grace. The local newspaper had just broken the story of fiscal mismanagement at a West Coast nonprofit clearinghouse that, ironically, provided services to help nonprofits manage their organizations more efficiently. The interim executive director responded, saying:

> "The time is not ripe to make any public statements. Given the many options [for reorganization], I am extremely confident that the services the nonprofit sector has been relying on for [27] years will continue." Despite his lengthy career in working with nonprofits, his reaction highlighted a glaring deficiency in his ability to deal effectively with the media. Five months after his pronouncement, he was forced to deal with the media again—this time to announce the closure of the clearinghouse. Community observers attributed the clearinghouse's problems to more than just a sluggish economy and increased competition. They suggested that the crisis scenario was probably hastened by management's errors of judgment. "I think the blame must lie somewhere in the building," said one observer. "They are not doing what they teach." (*San Francisco Chronicle,* January 22, 2004, and May 19, 2004)

It's Just a Matter of Time

According to www.merriam-webster.com, a crisis is defined as "an unstable or crucial time or state of affairs in which a *decisive change is impending; especially* one with the distinct possibility of a highly undesirable outcome" (emphasis added). From the moment that your organization experiences the onset of a crisis until services are returned to normal, you must be prepared to act. Crisis communication planning will facilitate the development of a rational response to a crisis.

Published reports provide these types of alarming headlines on a regular basis:

- *Nonprofit kept millions it collected for charity—Pipe Vine siphoned donations into company coffers for three years.* This headline refers to the scandal involving the United Way of the [San Francisco] Bay Area whose collection and distribution vendor, Pipeline, drew off millions of dollars to support overhead expenses.

- *United Way [Bay Area—CA] tweaked its financial reports—Accountants question charity's methods.* This is another headline from the same scandal alleging that the United Way board was aware of the financial malfeasance of its vendor.

- *Senator Seeks Financial Information from American Red Cross Leaders.* This headline refers to the Liberty Fund scandal that involved the American Red Cross's National Headquarters.

- *Ballet Company's database stolen containing donor credit card numbers.* This headline refers to an urban dance company whose database containing its donors' credit card numbers was stolen.

We hope your nonprofit will not ever experience any of these terrible events, but nevertheless, it can be plunged into a crisis by the malfunction of an office sprinkler system.

Nuts and Bolts of an Effective Crisis Communication Plan

An effective business continuity plan contains a crisis communication plan designed to convey important information while maintaining public trust. Your nonprofit needs to develop a plan that includes these important basics:

- *Trained spokespersons,* including a designated spokesperson and a back-up spokesperson. These individuals need to be skilled in communicating with media representatives and be available around the clock via their contact information. They should also be able to reach key staff at all times.

- *Materials that have been drafted in advance*—and are available at all times to the designated spokespersons. A fill-in-the-blanks prepared statement should be available at all times. The statement should include these talking points:
  - Name and address of the nonprofit
  - Mission of the nonprofit and the number of years the organization has been in existence
  - General language stating that as additional information becomes available, the nonprofit would share it with the media
  - Contact information for the nonprofit

- *Action plan for when a crisis occurs*

  When a crisis occurs, alert the designated spokesperson (who is informed by the Executive Director, a board member, or whoever is the senior person onsite at the time of the crisis) that an incident has occurred. Because it is important to be fully prepared before meeting with members of the media, the spokesperson needs to:
  - Determine *and confirm* the facts: who, what, why, where, when. The statement is always based on *confirmed* facts.
  - Always tell the truth. If the spokesperson doesn't know the answer, he or she needs to explain that the nonprofit is in the process of gathering all of the information. *The spokesperson should never invent a response.*
  - Update the media as the situation evolves.
  - Address the information needs of stakeholder groups, as part of the overall crisis communication plan. The spokesperson must determine the most appropriate way to brief board members, staff, volunteers, and clients.
  - Directing media inquiries

The crisis communication plan should also have protocols for interacting with media representatives. All media inquiries must be directed to the designated spokesperson, with no exceptions. Consequences must be imposed, including termination, for violating this rule. These consequences need to apply to volunteers as well as staff members.

In short, develop a plan that is streamlined yet addresses the most important issues in the crisis so that the nonprofit can move on to resume operations. Tell the truth—always—and reinforce the nonprofit's contributions to the community at large.

VALUE PROPOSITION OF BUSINESS CONTINUITY PLANNING

Preserving Your Nonprofit's Good Name

Business continuity planning is an important companion piece to risk management planning because each supports the fundamental deliverables of the other. In risk management planning, the current edition of the plan identifies those organizational areas that require attention to reduce the potential for frequency and severity of loss occurrences. In business continuity planning, the overall structure of the organization is examined and analyzed in order to develop backup systems, redundancies, and a road map for resuming operations in the event of a business interruption. Both plans:

- Rely on the transparency of organizational systems and procedures
- Facilitate a greater understanding of the workings of the organization by the board, management, staff, and volunteers
- Rely on knowing where the pressure points are within the organization, what the organizational vulnerabilities are, and what measures are being taken to strengthen the organization's internal controls

Designing a business continuity plan that includes a crisis communication plan is important in helping to preserve your nonprofit's good name in the event of a crisis. The better prepared that all of your non-profit's staff and volunteers are, the better they will perform in a crisis scenario. A crisis communication plan is essential in ensuring that your nonprofit's perspective is communicated to your local community and possibly the world.

Remaining a Viable Entity

Having an effective plan allows the nonprofit to remain a viable economic and operational entity, ready to serve regardless of what happens. In the event of a natural disaster that affects the broader community, such as earthquake or fire, the business continuity plan helps the nonprofit to continue to offer services to clients and provide support to clients and staff who may be impacted by the disaster.

Business continuity planning focuses on creating strategies to resume operations, such as establishing remote access to electronic documents and databases, and on building a depth of staffing so that key functional areas can be restored even if key staff members are not available. Staff members at organizations that have a business continuity plan feel confident that they will continue to have jobs regardless of the nature of the interruption.

A business continuity plan reduces the costs of resuming operations because a plan is in place that describes the sequence for resuming operations, the materials needed, contingency plans for an alternative work site, and the means by which electronic files will be accessed. An additional benefit is that the plan addresses Sarbanes-Oxley requirements and a number of best practices that are described in Chapter 9.

Preserving Stakeholder Confidence

The preparation of a risk management plan and a business continuity plan will enhance the nonprofit's image and credibility. Important stakeholders who will want to review these plans include auditors, insurance professionals, banks and other financial institutions, corporate partners, foundations, and high-wealth individuals. The synergy of having both plans in place communicates to stakeholders that the nonprofit is committed to taking a proactive approach to stewardship of its resources and to taking those actions necessary to ensure its financial viability for years to come.

LESSONS LEARNED FROM THE PRIVATE SECTOR

Large corporations, private companies, and small businesses have grappled with issues surrounding business continuity planning since the dawn of modern commerce. The information about business resumption that has emerged from the private sector, particularly since September 11, is instructive for nonprofits.

Important themes from these lessons include:

- Even with insurance coverage, a business will fail if it does not have a solid business continuity plan.

    Published studies show that over the past two decades, 78 percent of organizations that were insured but lacked contingency plans were not able to resume their operations on a long-term basis following a catastrophic loss of property and/or records. They found that customer loyalty, a trained workforce, and cash flow were gone within two years—despite the fact that many had business interruption coverage. (B2Bcontinuity.com)

- Everyone in the organization needs to know about crisis incident management and business resumption plans.

    Your nonprofit must understand that today's fast-paced business environment presents challenges in keeping staff and volunteers fully informed and prepared to engage in business continuity activities. Because turnover is so common in both the private and the nonprofit sector, many staff members will not be as conversant with security processes as they should be. Others, with detailed knowledge of security procedures, take that knowledge with them when they leave a nonprofit.

- Hope for the best and plan for the worst.

    Everyone in your nonprofit should understand what their role is when an emergency strikes. Security issues are important and need to be included in your nonprofit's business continuity plan. The sequence of your business resumption processes are crucial. Your nonprofit needs to ensure that those operational areas that need to be in place first are resumed first.

The plan to resume operations needs to be tested on a routine basis. Chapter 8 has recommendations for desktop exercises and emergency evacuation drills. Your nonprofit needs to thoroughly train staff and volunteers not only to deal with an immediate disaster, but to aid in the resumption of normal business operations.

Your staff and volunteers need to have experience in resuming operations and accessing backup files. Individuals assigned as "backup" to a key person must to try to resume operations in the division before disaster strikes. Experiential learning stays with adult learners longer than mere rote learning. The knowledge that a "backup" person gains from attempting to resume operations in a particular division will stay with him or her longer than would a simple lecture. Business resumption exercises should emphasize what needs to take place to re-start the nonprofit's essential operations and systems.

- Prepare for a community-wide disaster.

   The devastation of Hurricane Katrina illustrates the swath of destruction that can affect a city and its surroundings. If a disaster event of that magnitude hit your city, how would your nonprofit obtain the materials and resources it would need to resume operations? Are all of your key vendors located in your community? If so, your nonprofit should consider establishing relationships and opening accounts, if necessary, with vendors outside of your regional area. The vendors should be chosen with transportation of the merchandise in mind. The disaster scenario might destroy or damage the airport, so land transportation might be the only way to ship the goods.

   In the immediate aftermath of Hurricane Katrina, a number of corporations advertised in the media to request that staff members contact the company. Do your staff members know how to contact their supervisors in the event of a disaster? Do your staff members understand that they have an obligation to contact your nonprofit, even if it is just to tell you that they are not available? These types of expectations need to be made clear to staff as part of any business continuity plan. Staff members might not all be available, due to family obligations or personal injury or illness. Are there resources your nonprofit could use to obtain staff to temporarily or permanently replace your current staff?

- Write your nonprofit's business continuity plan to reflect your nonprofit's mission.

  As your nonprofit develops a business continuity plan, the overall structure needs to reflect the profile of the organization, its mission, its program, and its systemic configuration. The intent of a business continuity plan is to resume operations by accessing those systems that the nonprofit designed to sustain its internal controls.

  The plan needs to recognize that skillful handling of the crisis incident is an essential prerequisite to resuming operations. A team needs to be in place to handle the crisis incident, including media relations. A good crisis communication plan in key to a business continuity plan.

- Your nonprofit can benefit from an effective business continuity plan.

  The private sector has hailed business continuity planning as indispensable because of the types of benefits it provides to the company, its employees, and stakeholders. These benefits are easily translated into benefits for nonprofits.

  - The plan facilitates a safe and orderly recovery from a business interruption.
  - The plan helps staff members to react ways that are clear to them and to their colleagues and reduces the chance of mistakes and unfortunate decisions.
  - The plan will reduce the disruption of critical functions.
  - Emphasis on depth of staffing reduces reliance on certain key individuals who may be injured or killed in the disaster.

- Having a business continuity plan has the potential to reduce insurance premiums or assure renewal of coverage for business resumption and coverage of extra expenses.
- Most important, a good business continuity plan helps to protect your nonprofit's assets, staff, and volunteers.

Business continuity planning has been embraced by the private sector as essential to the stability and viability of companies around the world. Nonprofits can benefit from the difficult lessons that the private sector learned on September 11 and during Hurricane Katrina.

SUMMARY

Emergencies and business interruptions are a normal part of the life of any business or nonprofit. If a solid business continuity plan is in place, however, the incident does not need to destroy the nonprofit. The plan needs to include strategies for crisis communication, emergency response, and business resumption. Because the nonprofit's good name and credibility often are at stake in times of a crisis, investment in good business continuity planning pays dividends.

CHAPTER 6

Using the Business Continuity Planning Template

J oe Green is the executive Director of Delta House, a nonprofit that provides residential treatment at ten facilities to individuals in recovery from substance abuse. Two of the residents at one facility got into a heated argument, and one resident pushed the other out of a third-story window to the sidewalk below. Joe was at a conference 2,000 miles away at the time of the incident. The murder received extensive local media coverage. No one on his staff called Joe about the murder. When he returned to town, a board member called to say that she had heard about the murder. Needless to say, Joe was in a very difficult position.

BEGINNING TO PLAN: SOME CONSIDERATIONS

In Chapter 5 we examined what business continuity planning (BCP) is and the benefits it can bring to your nonprofit's operations. In this chapter we discuss the important principles and practices related to BCP and introduce the planning template. The first step in any business continuity plan is a visible commitment to it by the board and senior management. The tone at the top sets the stage for the level of commitment by the rest of the organization and the availability of resources needed to establish and maintain the plan. The board and senior management also need to be actively and visibly involved in the design, testing, and updating of the plan.

The plan should be prepared and assembled by a cross-functional team within your nonprofit to offer an array of perspectives on integrating operations. This business continuity planning team can include representatives from various departments; if your nonprofit is small, the team can include board, staff, and volunteers.

As you begin the preparation work for business continuity planning, consider these points:

- *Keeping everyone safe.* The plan needs to include specific protocols to help keep people safe—clients, staff, and visitors. Does everyone know where the exits are and how to evacuate the building/ care mobile in the event of an emergency?

- *Financing business resumption.* Without sufficient capital, it will be impossible to acquire the space and resources necessary to resume operations. Ensuring that adequate financial resources are in place to resume operations even at a different location is an essential component of a business continuity plan.

- *Impact of an emergency scenario at a neighboring office.* Consider how a business interruption at a neighboring building, office, or street could affect your operations. The interruption need not be directly in your nonprofit to affect access or your operations. Your offices could be subject to smoke or water damage. Your building could be "red-tagged" by the local building inspector, which means that, for the time, no one can go in or out of it. You would not be able to retrieve anything from your office, and you would be subject to legal consequences if you tried to gain entrance to the building.

- *Information technology infrastructure and remote access.* The sooner your nonprofit can access its electronic files, the sooner it will be able to resume operations. One of the most important steps you must take in business continuity planning is to establish viable backups to all electronic files and software and develop remote access to all electronic files, databases, e-mail, and software currently housed on your computers.

- *Family emergency preparedness.* Another issue to consider is how well your nonprofit's management, staff, and volunteers are prepared at home. Has each person developed a personal/home disaster preparedness plan?

- *Vendors and supplies.* Depending on the nature of your nonprofit's operations, your team might consider creating contingency plans for supplies, inventory, or other essentials. In the event of a community-wide disaster, your primary vendors may be affected. Have you established a business relationship with backup vendors—preferably in another city?

These issues are a just sampling of the types of concerns that your team would want to consider during the DIAD session. Begin to consider what makes your nonprofit unique. Your nonprofit's business continuity plan will need to reflect those unique aspects of your organizational structure, operations, or client base.

INTRODUCING THE BUSINESS CONTINUITY PLANNING TEMPLATE

The BCP template is an efficient tool for organizing the information needed to deal with a crisis and to take the steps to resume normal operations. In order to understand the design of the template, it is important to introduce it in a comprehensive fashionably including sections on crisis incident management, business resumption, and important information to access board, staff, volunteers, vendors, and other stakeholders. (See Exhibit 6.1.)

The cover of the plan should include the name and address of your nonprofit and the date that it was prepared. If your nonprofit has more than one office, the cover of the plan should indicate if the plan addresses only the main office, or if the plan addresses other locations. If the plan includes information relating to other offices, the addresses of these locations should be included.

Anyone who reads the plan should know when it was revised and any other information that would distinguish it from other documents in the

EXHIBIT 6.1   BUSINESS CONTINUITY PLAN

Business Continuity Plan for
[Name of the Nonprofit Organization (NPO)]
Address of Main Office
Telephone number
Fax number
Email and website

Crisis Incident Management Strategies

1. Crisis incident management leadership
2. Emergency situations
3. Crisis communications plan
4. Evacuation planning
5. Emergency fundraising
6. Determining the extent of damage
7. Nonprofit's expectations of staff and volunteers

Transitioning from Managing the Crisis Incident to Resuming Business Operations

Bridge to Business Resumption

Staff Availability

Financing Business Resumption

- Estimating the Cost of Recovery
- Sources of Financing

Determine Essential Business Functions

The BCP should have a summary of the essential functions, location of critical files, contacts and staff assignments for each of (your) NPO's functional areas.

- Executive and board.
- Administration.
- Human resources.
- Payroll.
- Finance operations.
- Client services.

EXHIBIT 6.1   BUSINESS CONTINUITY PLAN

- Information technology: Web site, -email, and Internet access.
- Development and fundraising.

In this section, **each of the management functions** will be presented to highlight:

- Operational priorities.
- Financing the business resumption.
- Depth of staffing. Equipment, materials, and software.
- Reports or other deadline items.
- Public sector contacts.
- Private sector contacts.
- Location of essential documents and files.
- Staff and board contact information.

Vendors

Be sure to include all important vendors including ones in these categories:

- Utilities: phone, gas/oil, water, sewer
- IT, computer supplies, hardware, and software
- Payroll and other vendors of outsourced functions
- Handyman or contractor
- Automotive repair
- Lock and key
- Glass replacement
- Elevator
- 24-hour emergency numbers for the local government

Working At an Alternative Location

- Mutual support agreement(s) with other NPOs or neighborhood organizations
- Basic inventory of furnishings and equipment to resume operations at an alternative location
- Commercial real estate requirements

Timetable for updating the Business Continuity Plan

nonprofit's collection. The names of the plan's team members would be helpful as well.

Part I Crisis Incident Management

The first part of the plan should address how your nonprofit will deal with a crisis scenario. If your nonprofit experiences an emergency, natural disaster, or business interruption, you will need to deal with the crisis aspects *first* before you can consider resuming operations. Maintaining the nonprofit's good name and image hinges on how skillfully management handles a crisis scenario. The nonprofit's stakeholders and the public expect the nonprofit to be decisive, competent, and forthright in its strategy for managing a crisis and moving forward.

Consider, in the aftermath of Hurricane Katrina, the difference between the initial Coast Guard response, which saved thousands of lives, and the initial FEMA response. Political considerations may have tainted overall public perception, but the numbers tell the story. The public saw a president who was shocked by what he saw, a mayor in great emotional pain, a political appointee who was overwhelmed by the task of heading FEMA, and, finally, the calm, steady know-how of a Coast Guard admiral whose genius for logistics and strategy was first illustrated in the rescue of thousands trapped in lower Manhattan on September 11th. These were the faces and the actions that defined this country's response at that moment in time. We hope your nonprofit will never have to endure anything as horrendous as Hurricane Katrina or a terrorist attack. But when your staff, clients, donors, and community look back at your nonprofit's response to a crisis, what do you want them to remember?

As you craft your nonprofit's objectives for crisis management, consider two important elements: people's safety and well-being and a solid crisis communication plan. Consider your nonprofit's programmatic profile and methods of generating revenue. To remain a viable entity, your nonprofit will need to begin operations immediately following a business interruption. The objectives of your nonprofit's crisis incident management will center around those results that keep people safe, convey necessary and sufficient information, and execute strategies to resume operations.

Crisis Incident Management Strategies

The actual management of a crisis scenario begins by developing seven strategies (in advance of any crisis through your business continuity planning) that address:

1. Crisis incident management leadership
2. Emergency situations
3. Crisis communications plan
4. Evacuation planning
5. Emergency fundraising
6. Determining the extent of damage
7. Nonprofit's expectations of staff and volunteers

Crisis Incident Management Leadership

Everyone in your nonprofit must be aware of who is in charge in an emergency. In addition, at least one backup leader must be identified for this leadership assignment. The executive director may seem a logical choice, but in an emergency, this individual will be swamped with other obligations, including putting a public "face" on the nonprofit. The plan should identify those individuals and backups who will coordinate the nonprofit's disaster response and subsequent business resumption.

Board leadership in managing the crisis scenario is also crucial. The board needs to prepare for a crisis in advance by fully participating in business continuity planning and by preparing documents, such as emergency protocols for financial management, that can be triggered in the event of an emergency.

The team that is working directly to create the business continuity plan is the primary link to those who are assembling a business continuity task force that will facilitate crisis incident management and business resumption. The task force can include key managers within the nonprofit as well as members of the board's executive committee.

Emergency Situations

The chart in Exhibit 6.2 illustrates an array of emergency situations and how to deal with each one. As part of the ongoing staff training in dealing with emergencies, it is important for everyone to consider the best course(s) of action associated with each emergency. Does everyone in the nonprofit know where first aid kits are kept? Does everyone know how to operate a fire extinguisher? Fire extinguishers vendors often have training models that can be brought to the workplace and used to train everyone on safe and appropriate fire extinguisher use.

The nonprofit should also have flashlights and other safety equipment readily available in the event of a power outage. Staff and volunteers should know what happens in the office when the power goes out. Some buildings have emergency fire doors that automatically close in the event of a power outage. If this is the case in your building, staff and volunteers should know how to open these doors to evacuate from the office.

Crisis Communications Plan

The need for a well-crafted crisis communication plan was first examined in Chapter 5. As part of your nonprofit's business continuity plan, it is essential to document the crisis communications strategy and execution by first identifying communication patterns; for example, how do staff members communicate with their supervisors, colleagues, board members, and other stakeholders? The plan must have separate communication strategies for each stakeholder group, but determining in advance the types of information that are necessary and sufficient is crucial to the success of the plan. The communications plan—a phone tree or some other type of calling pattern that you have prepared as part of your nonprofit's business continuity planning—should ensure that your nonprofit's staff and volunteers can get in touch with the executive team in the immediate aftermath of a crisis or emergency.

Communication among the nonprofit's management, board, staff, and volunteers is essential in an emergency situation. The plan recommends several approaches to better communication.

| EXHIBIT 6.2 | CONTINUUM OF EMERGENCY SITUATIONS | |

Emergency	Initial Action	Follow-Up
Rolling blackout	Turn off all lights and electrical equipment to prevent a power surge when power is restored. Leave 1 light in "on" mode to determine when power is restored. Activate flashlights and battery-operated radios.	Develop list of tasks that do not require computer support, such as filing.
Medical	Call the main desk and request 911 be contacted. Describe the emergency situation Stay calm and gather available medical information to be given to emergency personnel	First aid and CPR training for staff on an annual basis.
Fire in another office in building housing your offices	Alert the main desk and ensure that 911 has been contacted.	Perform head count at gathering site. Report names of individuals not accounted for to firefighting authorities. Cooperate with fire-fighters and emergency personnel.
Fire	Alert the main desk and ensure that 911 has been contacted. Remain calm. Note your location on the evacuation map. Move in an orderly fashion toward the stairs and exit the building. Close all doors as you exit. Don't use elevators. Once outside, move away from the building.	Perform head count at gathering site. Report names of individuals not accounted for to firefighting authorities.

Continues

EXHIBIT 6.2   *CONTINUED*

Emergency	Initial Action	Follow-up
Criminal activity and workplace violence	Alert the main desk or a supervisor.	Report suspicious activity immediately. Take threats of violence seriously and report them to management.
Earthquake	Stay calm, and "duck and cover." Stay clear of tall objects and window. Stay under cover until the initial shocks have subsided.	Meet in the designated area. Ensure that staff, clients and others in the office are accounted for. Advise emergency personnel if anyone is missing.

- *Phone tree.* A phone tree is a structured plan that features specific calling patterns for identified leaders. The crisis management team leader puts the phone tree into play. Everyone who has obligations to make phone calls knows in advance whom to call. The phone tree must have up-to-date contact information and also should have alternative phone numbers for each person, perhaps including family members' contact information. For example, Mary Smith's home phone and cell phone could be listed, but her husband's cell phone could be listed as an alternative number. The nonprofit needs to assure staff members that the alternative numbers will never be used unless: (1) there is an emergency and (2) the staff member could not be reached via the primary number.

- *If the nonprofit has an 800 number,* that number should be given to the board, staff, and volunteers in the event of an emergency. The number could have a recording that provides information on the nature of the crisis, alternative location of the offices, and other information that callers would need.

- *Web site.* The nonprofit's Web site can be a source for information and a conduit for emergency donations. Include the Web address in all press releases so that the public can contact the nonprofit.

Crisis Management Team Staffing

The leaders of the crisis management team should be known to board, staff, and volunteers well in advance of a crisis. Contact information for the team should be disseminated as soon as the team is formed and updated at regular intervals. The executive director may or may not be the leader of the team, particularly if he or she is not in town at the time of the crisis. The board and staff do need to know who is leading the crisis management team at the time of the crisis incident. A set of protocols need to be in place to announce the name of the Crisis Management Team leader. The board and staff should be contacted immediately with this information. Similarly, the plan should also identify the backup leader of the board in the event that the board chair or other members of the executive committee are not available.

Media Relations

The "media relations" section of the business continuity plan describes how to execute this important part of crisis incident management. Cultivating good media relations is essential in advance of any emergency situation. The media should have the name(s) and contact information for the nonprofit's spokespersons. These are the "go to" individuals who can provide the media with the most accurate information at any given moment.

The media relations plan should also include:

- *A good press release.* Prior to an emergency, it is important to have the outline of a prepared statement ready so that the nonprofit's spokesperson can simply "fill in the blanks." The information relevant to the crisis or emergency can be inserted to make the statement available at a moment's notice. Because public perception of your nonprofit is directly correlated to the credibility and professionalism that your nonprofit displays, it might be beneficial to arrange media training for the nonprofit's designated spokesperson.

- *Media contacts.* The template has a section in which your nonprofit can list important media contacts. The crisis management team must be trained to handle media inquiries and in how to establish a productive relationship with the media in advance of a crisis incident. Having a clear set of procedures for crisis communications is important; these procedures include training the staff and volunteers to refer all media inquiries to the nonprofit's spokesperson. Consequences for failure to abide by these procedures should be clearly explained to staff and volunteers and, if necessary, be carried out swiftly and visibly. The intent of such a policy is to safeguard the image of the nonprofit.

- *Communication with other stakeholders.* Your nonprofit's crisis communication plan should also include specific strategies for conveying information that is necessary and sufficient to each of these stakeholder groups:

  - *Clients.* Clients should receive information about where to obtain services, whether the nonprofit's current programmatic offerings are impacted by the crisis and to what extent, and where to call to obtain further information. This information can be disseminated via the nonprofit's website, public service announcements on radio or TV or via a designated phone number.

  - *Volunteers.* Volunteers should be advised of the types of assistance that the nonprofit needs at the moment, how to get in touch with the volunteer coordinator—volunteers need the name of the person and the phone number—and what other expectations the nonprofit has in terms of volunteer service.

  - *Vendors.* Vendors need to know where the nonprofit is currently operating and how to get in touch with the individual(s) handling vendor inquiries.

  - *Financial institutions.* Banks, stock brokerages, and other financial institutions will want to know where the nonprofit is currently conducting business, names of individuals who are authorized to transact business, and whether any board protocols on emergency financial operations have been triggered. Remember, the financial institutions will want to see documents and have documentation in place (i.e., signatures) prior to the crisis incident for any individuals who would be authorized to transact business. Remember, to protect the interests of the nonprofit, banks and other financial institutions are limited by written instructions regarding who is authorized to do business them.

- *Public.* Public inquiries need to be addressed by means of a general statement providing information on how to contact the nonprofit, the contact information for the spokespersons or their designees, and information on how to make a donation. The nonprofit can utilize their website or media reports to respond to general inquiries.

Evacuation Planning

Keeping people safe is a primary objective in evacuation planning. A good evacuation plan needs to be in place in the event of an emergency, —and everyone on the staff needs to know how to get out of the building and where to meet. Accounting for all of the staff, volunteers, clients, and anyone else on the nonprofit's premises at the time of the crisis incident is crucial. Emergency responders must be told if someone is missing. Having routine fire drills or emergency evacuation drills helps to ensure the safety of everyone on the nonprofit's premises.

Sample Evacuation Plans from the Template

There Has Been a Crisis Incident at Your Nonprofit.
What Should You Do?
Evacuation Procedures—Your business continuity plan should include specific instructions on evacuation procedures.

1. Identify stairways, doors, or other emergency exits. [Floor plans should be posted in strategic areas of your offices. The floor plans should clearly identify the closest exits.]
2. Specify a location where all staff, volunteers, clients, visitors are to meet so that the management team can do a head count. [Identify a primary meeting place and an alternate meeting place for your nonprofit's staff and volunteers.]

3. Establish protocols to assist police, firefighters, and other emergency personnel. [The protocols could include a listing of the office locations for individuals who have physical challenges, such as mobility or visual impairment.]

In the event of a fire:

Evacuate the building and relocate through stairwells, *not elevators,* to the ground floor. There should be a special location designated for individuals who have physical mobility challenges. Firefighters would be advised of this operation to begin their rescue operations. If your building has an intercom system, be sure that the emergency announcement can be heard on all floors and in all offices.

- Alert everyone and ask them to remain calm but move quickly. In an emergency, every moment counts. The calmer that the staff, volunteers, and visitors remain, the faster they can evacuate the building. Once everyone has evacuated the building, a headcount will take place and firefighters will be advised of the number of individuals not accounted for and where these people might be located in the building.

- Listen for instructions and report to the designated emergency exits. Staff and volunteers should be trained ahead of any crisis situation to do this.

- Everyone has to be accounted for before anyone—member of staff, volunteer, visitor, or whomever—is permitted to leave the premises. The crisis management team must have a list of individuals who have been accounted for, a list of those who were not in the building that day, and a list of those who have not been accounted for. The team should give this list to the fire captain so that emergency responders will have an idea of how many people may still be in the building. *Staff and volunteers should understand that full cooperation with the census-taking is mandatory and that failure to cooperate may result in disciplinary action.*

- Go to the emergency meeting place. Actually, there should be two emergency meeting places. If, for some reason, it is not safe to congregate at the primary meeting place, everyone needs to know where the alternative meeting place is. As part of the disaster drills, staff and volunteers should occasionally be directed to gather at the alternative meeting place.

- Keep clear of the building to avoid falling debris. Once staff and volunteers have assembled in the meeting place and are accounted for, it they must understand to keep a safe distance from the building and stay out of the way of emergency responders. Once out of the buildings, staff and volunteers should know that they are prohibited from returning to the building until the "all clear" signal is given.

In case of a power outage:
If you are in the elevator at the time of a power outage, remain calm and follow these instructions:

- Push the button to sound the buzzer alarm in the elevator.
- Open the phone box and follow the instructions.
- Use emergency phones flashlights, portable radios, and batteries, and give the location and features of emergency equipment.
- The Executive Director or designee or the individual first seeing smoke or the fire should ensure that an alarm has been sounded and that the staff, volunteers, and clients know that they must evacuate the building. Follow the evacuation plan and exit the building immediately.

These evacuation plans are examples of the types of plans that should be a part of your nonprofit's crisis incident management strategy. Chapter 8 will present strategies for practicing emergency drills and for helping your staff learn how to evacuate your nonprofit's facilities in variety of emergency situations.

Emergency Fundraising

We live in a very generous society. An important part of your nonprofit's business continuity plan is a clear strategy for accepting and acknowledging emergency donations. Donation offers are not always financial. There should be plans in place to accept emergency donations of time, talent, and money. Consider a protocol to accept emergency cash donations online. Your Web site needs to have a secure method for online donations that includes encryption and other protection against hackers. If your nonprofit has not established its own secure system to accept online donations, it should consider outsourcing this important function. Ensure that there is also a procedure in place to acknowledge these donations.

- *Leveraging media interest.* An important part of the nonprofit's media relations is having a strategy for leveraging media interest to communicate needs and information on how to make a donation. This information should be included in the generic press release. If the situation does not warrant this type of a request, the language can be deleted.

- *Procedures for accepting and processing emergency donations* (Internet, mail, in-person, over the phone). A member of the crisis management team needs to be in charge of the emergency fundraising. This individual needs to put into place the procedures outlined in the business continuity plan to accept, process, and acknowledge emergency donations. This person would also be responsible for activating the online emergency donations feature and working with the vendor for this service.

- *Procedures for acknowledging emergency donations.* The emergency fundraising portion of the nonprofit's business continuity plan needs to include procedures for providing prompt acknowledgment of cash and in-kind donations, in writing on the nonprofit's letterhead. Be sure to incorporate the individuals who contributed into the nonprofit's donor base.

Determining the Extent of Damage

The crisis management team needs to begin assessing any physical damage to the nonprofit's building or other property and establishing a logical sequence for repairs as soon as possible following the crisis. This triage method will help to prioritize tasks into a progression that leads to the restoration of operations.

If the crisis relates to a personnel matter, such as a criminal act perpetrated by a member of the nonprofit's staff or volunteers, then the team needs to begin assessing the extent of the damage to the nonprofit's good name, public image, and other intangibles. A plan should be crafted to restore the good name of the nonprofit.

Nonprofit's Expectations of Staff and Volunteers

Your nonprofit needs to be clear about what it expects from staff and volunteers in the event of a crisis or emergency. Staff members may be called on to work hours that are different from their normal work times, or to work in shifts. Volunteers may be asked to help with additional tasks. Although staff members may be advised that new work expectations and hours are conditions of their employment, volunteers are under no obligation to undertake additional tasks.

Other expectations would include abiding by the nonprofit's policy to direct all media inquiries to the designated spokesperson. The nonprofit needs to be very clear about the rationale for this policy and the consequences for noncompliance. The policy should be shared with staff and volunteers as a normal part of their orientation curriculum and in routine in-service sessions that review the procedures and expectations in the event of an emergency. Staff and volunteers alike are covered by this policy and are subject to the same consequences, which might include termination.

Staff and volunteers could also be involved in emergency fundraising. Those persons assigned to this area need to be screened carefully in advance. Before they begin their assignments, they need to be briefed on the scope of their work; the potential impact that their words, actions, and behavior could have on the nonprofit's good name; and what is expected in terms of schedule and productivity.

Part II Transitioning from Managing the Crisis Incident to Resuming Business Operations

Bridge to Business Resumption

As your nonprofit works through the crisis incident management, the crisis management team needs to begin to move as quickly as possible to resuming normal operations. This section of the business continuity plan serves to facilitate the timely resumption of operations. The plan should have a summary of the nonprofit's essential functions; location of critical files; contacts; and staff assignments for each of the nonprofit's functional areas.

To begin the process of business resumption, the nonprofit needs to know how many staff members are available to return to work. Depending on the nature of the emergency, staff members may be injured or dead, or have family members who need care. If the emergency is community-wide, such as a hurricane or earthquake, people may have transportation problems as well. The staff availability checklist (see Exhibit 6.3) is designed to help the nonprofit's management determine the well-being and work readiness of its staff. The questions are straightforward, but use of the form will enable managers to gather a consistent level of information to make staffing decisions. The annotated form that follows describes the rationale for the information requested.

Staff Availability Checklist

Active Phone Number: This number may not be the home or cell phone number that the nonprofit has on record, but it is the number where the staff member can be reached.

Present Residence Address: Similarly, this address may be a temporary address, but for the purposes of business resumption, it is an address that the staff member may prefer that the nonprofit uses.

Home E-mail: If the nonprofit's e-mail is not available, using a personal e-mail address may be the only way that the nonprofit can contact the staff member.

Any injuries to staff member? If the staff member is injured, he or she may need to work abbreviated shifts or work from home. If the injury is severe, the worker may need to go on short-term or long-term disability.

If yes, nature of injury: The nature of the injury may require a doctor's recommendation in terms of whether the staff member needs to be assigned light duties.

EXHIBIT 6.3 STAFF AVAILABILITY CHECKLIST

Staff Member Name: _____

Department: _____

Active Phone Number: _____

Present Residence Address: _____

Home E-mail: _____

Any injuries to staff member?   ❐ yes ❐ no

If yes, nature of injury

_____

Any injuries to family member?   ❐ yes ❐ no

If yes, nature of injury:

_____

Any serious damage to staff member's property?   ❐ yes ❐ no

_____

Best times for this staff person to work his or her shift:

_____

Any time this staff person could not work:

_____

Why?

_____

Transportation: Does this person have transportation? _____

Can this person assist others in getting to work?

_____

Does the staff member need any assistance? _____

Any injuries to family member? The staff member may be dealing with the care of one or more family members.

If yes, nature of injury.

Any serious damage to staff member's property? The staff member may be dealing with damage to his or her property, or issues related to filing insurance claims for the damage.

Best times for this staff person to work his or her shift: It is important for staff members to understand that until operations are fully resumed, they may have to work different hours or in shifts.

Any time this staff person could not work: Although in the short term, the nonprofit might be in a position to pressure a staff member to return to work, taking a reasoned approach would provide more positive results.

Transportation: Does this person have transportation? Can this person assist others in getting to work? This information can be useful in arranging for carpools or other forms of transportation for groups of staff members.

Does the staff member need any assistance? Determining if the staff member requires assistance is important in maintaining positive relations with the person as well as facilitating his or her return to work.

Financing Business Resumption

Securing the financing to resume operations is crucial to successful business resumption. Although this information needs to be documented, the data contained in this section is highly confidential and should *not* be included in the copies of the business continuity plan that are distributed to the general staff.

Estimating the Cost of Recovery

Use this portion of the plan to identify what your nonprofit would need to resume operations in terms of equipment, space, and the sources of funds that will facilitate resumption of operations. Although it is not possible to know in advance what the actual cost of recovery will be, having inventories of furniture and information technology equipment can be very useful in arranging for temporary or permanent replacement of these essentials.

Sources of Financing

Your nonprofit will need to consider what resources it has to finance business resumption. These resources could include:

- *Insurance.* Insurance claims could pay for repairs to your offices, replace furnishings and equipment, and pay for additional expenses associated with business resumption.

- *Line of credit.* A line of credit needs to be accessible immediately and should reflect the level of funding that would be necessary to resume operations in another location.

- *Other sources.* Your nonprofit may have investments or money market funds or other financial instruments that could be used for business resumption.

Determine Essential Business Functions

When clients are asked to describe the nonprofit's essential business functions, many look puzzled and respond that *everything* they do is essential. That's not quite true. Some functions, such as payroll, finance, and information technology (IT) take precedence over other functions, such as volunteer administration. Essential business functions are those functional areas that your nonprofit will need to restore first before the rest of its operations can be fully restored. What business activities and functions are essential for your nonprofit? Who performs these activities and functions? Are there staff trained to back up the individuals who are tasked with performing essential functions? Are there written protocols and procedures for these activities and functions? Some examples of essential functions include:

- *Executive and board.* This component of the nonprofit's function is the central nervous system of the organization—and the leader in managing the crisis aspect of the interruption as well as the business resumption.

- *Administration.* This function coordinates activities and ensures that the business continuity plan is executed as planned.

- *Human resources.* This function has an important role to plan in ensuring that the essential functions are staffed. If the nonprofit has to relocate temporarily or permanently, human resources is the function that facilitates scheduling of and assigning staff members to the important tasks related to the resumption of operations.

- *Payroll.* Payroll is an essential function because, particularly during an emergency, staff members need to be issued their customary salary without interruption.

- *Finance operations.* This component is essential. The nonprofit cannot resume operations if it cannot take in revenue and pay for necessary expenses.

- *Client services.* This function may be modified or scaled back during a business interruption, but if client services form part of the nonprofit's mission, then clients must be served in some form during the business resumption stage.

- *Information technology: Web site, e-mail, and Internet access.* Nonprofits live and die by their computers and IT systems, including e-mail, Internet access, and the organization's Web site. The Web site can be used as a resource for conveying important messages to staff, volunteers, and clients and the public at large. *The faster a nonprofit can access its electronic resources (i.e. software, files, and databases), the faster it can resume normal operations.*

- *Development and fundraising.* For many nonprofits, development and fundraising are the primary methods of generating revenue to support programs and overhead. In the event of a business interruption, it is essential that this function not only continue, but also be expanded to address the needs created by the nature of the interruption.

In this section of the plan, your nonprofit will need to list *each of the key management functions* and identify the people and resources needed to resume operations. Begin this process by establishing goals and milestones for the next 24, 48, and 72 hours. To do this, management might consider developing simple daily agendas to outline what it wants to have accomplished by the end of any given day. This information should be disseminated to staff and key board members.

To establish a timeline and sequence for business resumption, consider how each of these factors would contribute to the speed of your nonprofit's business resumption:

- *Operational priorities.* What tasks must be completed every day, every week, and every month? Payroll, for example, might need to be prepared by the close of business every Wednesday. If this function is outsourced, the vendor may need the data by the close of business every Tuesday. Clearly, payroll is one of the functions that is a top priority. Staff members and their families are counting on their paychecks to maintain their family life. If the emergency reflects a community-wide disaster, then staff members will need their paychecks more than ever.

- *Financing the business resumption.* Give high priority to the activities necessary to trigger the funding to resume business operations. After an emergency that has resulted in damage or loss, contact the nonprofit's insurance professional immediately. If the nonprofit needs to be housed in another location temporarily or permanently, a line of credit may be triggered to pay for rent, equipment, and other extra expenses that may or may not be covered by insurance. This funding may be necessary to cover expenses while the nonprofit is waiting for the claim to be paid.

- *Depth of staffing.* For each of the critical functions, identify key personnel as well as those staff members who have been trained to step in if the key person(s) is not available.

- *Equipment, materials, and software.* Document whatever is needed to complete the operational priorities to indicate what is needed to resume operations for each function. In this way, if the nonprofit's offices have been destroyed or are not accessible, there is a more specific (i.e. limited) list of equipment, materials, and software that corresponds to critical functions. For this reason, it is very important to document IT functions, such as how to access backup electronic files, Web sites, databases, and software.

- *Reports or other deadline items.* An important report or proposal may be due in a very short time. This document may become a priority item in the agenda.

- *Public sector contacts.* The nonprofit should have a list of the government agencies that it is in contact with on a routine basis, including emergency contact numbers. This list should also include utilities, such as electricity, water, and phone service .as well as fuel sources for heat.

- *Private sector contacts.* This list should include companies and businesses with which your nonprofit might have a collaborative relationship or stakeholders, such as banks and financial institutions.

- *Location of essential documents and files.* Your nonprofit should have a master list of important documents and their location, even if these documents are stored electronically. This master list can be stored on a PDA, CD or other electronic storage. The master list should be stored off site as well as in several strategic locations within the nonprofit. The board's executive committee should also have copies of the master list. *As part of any business continuity planning, your nonprofit needs to establish a viable means to backup software, databases, and documents on a daily basis. These electronic materials need to be stored off site. Web-based services are now available at reasonable prices.*

- *Staff and board contact information.* This information should include pagers and cell phone numbers.

Vendors

Vendors play an important role in resuming operations. Maintaining contact with a vendor can be difficult if the current supply chain is compromised by a community-wide disaster. Having an "emergency order" on file with suppliers of IT equipment, hardware, and software could save your nonprofit time and, possibly, money. It is equally important to identify a backup vendor for your critical needs, such as IT, office supplies, hardware/software, payroll, and emergency needs, such as glass, lock and key, and contractors.

Include at least the following information for each vendor in your business continuity plan.

- Vendor name
- Contact person at vendor (Include this person's cell phone number)
- Phone number, cellphone, email and website of the business
- Fax number
- Your nonprofit's account number
- Name of person and alternate at your nonprofit who is authorized to place an order

Important! Be sure to compile listings of these categories of vendors in addition to other suppliers. Be sure to list your nonprofit's account number or other identifying data on the same sheet as the contact number for each vendor.

Here are some examples of categories of vendors:

- Utilities: phone, gas/oil, water, sewer
- IT, computer supplies, hardware, and software
- Payroll and other vendors of outsourced functions
- Handyman or contractor
- Automotive repair
- Lock and key
- Glass replacement
- Elevator
- 24-hour emergency numbers for the local government

Working at an Alternative Location

Your nonprofit's office may not be available for an extended period of time. In order to resume operations in a timely manner, you might have to relocate temporarily or even permanently. For the immediate short term, it is useful to have mutual support agreement(s) with other nonprofits or neighborhood organizations that would have space available to accommodate limited operations.

An important addition to your nonprofit's business continuity plan is an inventory of furnishings and equipment that are necessary to resume operations at an alternative location. Having your commercial real estate requirements on file with your nonprofit's commercial real estate broker is useful for permanent relocation needs.

ESTABLISHING A TIMETABLE FOR UPDATING THE BUSINESS CONTINUITY PLAN

In the months immediately after the drafting of the nonprofit's business continuity plan, follow-on deliverables will be added to the original plan. Review the first draft of the plan in three to four months and then again in three months to ensure that the follow-on deliverables have been incorporated. It is particularly important to ensure that those deliverables are crafted in a user-friendly manner and have been tested via a desktop exercise. Desktop exercises are presented in Chapter 8. After the first year, review the business continuity plan every six months.

SUMMARY

Using a template to create a business continuity plan can help a nonprofit to develop solid plans for managing a crisis and resuming business operations. It can also help the organization learn more about the ways in which each of the critical functions depends on the others and how the nonprofit functions overall. The knowledge that comes from this type of planning is fundamental to crafting a business continuity plan that will be successful for the organization.

CHAPTER 7

Done in a Day Session for Business Continuity Planning

One of the important aspects of business continuity planning is ensuring that information vital to the resumption of operations is included in the plan. A challenge to this process is ensuring that proprietary information is available on a need to know basis.

The consultants were meeting with the Blue Sky Center's Business Continuity Planning Team. The meeting's primary deliverable was to jump-start the process. The size of the planning team—23 people—was much too large. Planning had become mired in bureaucratic process. As the consultants began to facilitate the meeting, they attempted to refocus the group's attention on information that was essential in business continuity planning. They asked about the strategies that might already be in place to resume financial operations. The chief financial officer cheerfully replied, "I'm the only one in this entire organization who knows the bank codes to transact business." The consultant replied, "And a long life to you, sir!"

HOW TO PREPARE FOR THE DIAD SESSION

Success in any Done in a Day (DIAD) planning is contingent on the quality of preparation. The more complete the preparation, the faster the progress in assembling the first edition of a plan. Tthe suggestions that follow can help you save time, energy, and money.

- *Assemble a business continuity planning team.* Select high-quality people to be on the team who are very knowledgeable about one or more of the nonprofit's organizational components, particularly as these components and their functions are integrated. Just as your nonprofit did in its risk management planning, select a team of the nonprofit's star "players" for the first round of business continuity planning. If your nonprofit is small, the business continuity planning team can be a blend of staff, key volunteers, and board members. This type of blending can reap benefits in the eventual dissemination of learning that comes from business continuity planning. Ensure that the team has sufficient resources to produce a quality plan, even if that means shifting workloads or delaying delivery of projects. The team should also receive small perks for their work on this project. The perks need not be elaborate or expensive but should be something that the individual team member would enjoy—perhaps a gift card to a coffee shop or one week's reserved parking in a prime location or even a prepaid ticket for public transportation in your area (e.g., a $10 rail pass).

- *Assemble only that information which is necessary and sufficient.* One of the biggest challenges that nonprofits face in assembling their first business continuity plan is "data dump"—staff members believe that more is better in terms of the volume of information that is brought to the plan. Emphasize that material is not useful unless it is relevant. Make sure that the team focuses on that information your nonprofit will need in the first 24 hours, 48 hours, and first week. The rest of the information should be accessible via the electronic storage/archive system that your nonprofit uses.

- *Be aware of hidden and not so hidden barriers.* The barriers to business continuity planning are similar if not identical to the barriers discussed for risk management planning. Resolve to push through these barriers too. Refuse to accept the excuse that not all of the committee members are available on the date chosen for the DIAD session. Insist on mandatory attendance, and arrange for other obligations to be handled by a substitute. Team members need to be fully onboard with business continuity planning, just as the team was for risk management planning. Ensure that business continuity planning has the same level of full and visible endorsement of the board and senior management as did the risk management planning. Be prepared for the possibility that a member of the team will be ill on the day of the planning. The team needs to have backup staff and/or volunteers who have assisted in the preparation of the materials that will be included in the business continuity plan and can stand in for an absent member during the DIAD session.

- *The better prepared you are, the better the quality of planning for the DIAD session.* Consider the types of data and materials that would need to be brought to the DIAD session, and develop a strategy for assigning the team members to prepare those materials.

    Important! Because of the sensitivity of some of the information that needs to be included in a business continuity plan, it is important to ensure that the plan is drafted at two levels of detail: an executive version, which contains proprietary information, and a more basic version for staff and volunteers, which emphasizes what is necessary and sufficient in terms of information.

- *Consider how the template can be used in an overall business continuity planning educational piece for the organization's board, staff, and volunteers.* To implement a business continuity plan, you must train the DIAD team and the nonprofit's board, staff, and volunteers. You can simplify training by following the template. A sample training outline is included in this chapter.

- *Consider asking your insurance professional, financial professional, information technology professional, and/or legal professional to sit in on at least part of the DIAD session for feedback and input.* Just as in risk management planning, the nonprofit's professional advisors are excellent sources of guidance in the design and content of your business continuity plan. These individuals may not be available for the entire DIAD session but probably would be willing to sit in on part of the session or review the plan that was assembled from the session. These professionals know your nonprofit's needs, intricacies, and challenges. They can also help you to leverage your business continuity plan for additional benefits. Chapter 9 reviews the types of benefits that can be garnered from an effective plan.

Timetable Frame for Preparation

Because preparation is key to success, consider these steps in the period leading up to the DIAD for business continuity planning.

Three Weeks in Advance

- Choose the date and book the room. Work to ensure that as many key players are available that day, but choose a date and stick to it! It is particularly important to have a backup person who fully participates in the prep and the planning for each key player. (Such backups will be needed for the business continuity plan anyway.)

- Identify the staff and/or volunteers, including board members, who should be seated on the first business continuity planning committee. These individuals need not be senior management, but all need to be highly competent self-starters. Everyone on the team will be a "backup" to another member. The individuals should be advised that they are required to attend the DIAD session and to participate fully in the brief preparatory work. Team members also need to know that on the day of the DIAD session, they will not have access to cell phones and pagers. They need to advise family that emergency phone calls must go to the receptionist (or person designated as such that day).

- Engage a facilitator for the session. The individual should be knowledgeable about organizational behavior and, if possible, about business continuity planning or insurance. The individual can be a senior executive or member of the board or an outside consultant. The facilitator should be given a copy of the template, worksheets, and any other documents that you will want to use to construct the first edition of the business continuity planning plan. The facilitator should understand that the DIAD session is the launch of an ongoing business continuity planning program. As part of the DIAD session, the dates of upcoming rounds of risk assessment, business continuity planning strategies, and evaluation should be selected.

Two Weeks in Advance

Use the checklists and questionnaires that follow to gather information and data that must be included in the nonprofit's business continuity plan.

Important! If a worksheet, questionnaire, or topic doesn't apply, ignore it for now. Don't waste time in prolonged analysis; just concentrate on gathering the information and documents.

Business Continuity Planning Preparation Worksheets

The following checklists and worksheets are samples of the types of materials that your nonprofit could use in preparing for the DIAD session.

IT and Telecommunications Infrastructure

This list is intended to help your team develop a list of the information technology (IT) and telecommunications equipment (including software and hardware) that is essential to resume operations. This list does not address specific strategies for backing up your current electronic files. Those strategies are addressed in business resumption planning.

For all categories that are relevant to your nonprofit, include the description, identifying information, or model number.

- Primary IT vendors (names and contact information):
  - Alternative vendor if the primary vendor is not available (names and contact information).

- Telephone system description and vendor.
  - Can the vendor arrange for immediate forwarding of incoming calls to an 800 number or stand-alone voice mail?
- Number of desktop computers.
- Number of laptops.
- Do you have a server?
  - Is server located on site? (yes or no)
  - Do you have a backup server?
- How often are electronic files and databases backed up? Describe the method and the location where the backups are stored.
- Have you tested the backup to ensure that it is operational?
- Approximate number of accessories (i.e., zip drives, printers, etc.).
- Databases.
  - Type of database used for financial operations.
  - Type of database used for development and fundraising.
  - Types of software used for office operations.
  - Contact information for your Internet service provider, including your nonprofit's account number and any other identifying information, and your e-mail provider.
  - Webmaster (name and contact information).
  - Web hosting service (name and contact information).
  - Domain name ownership.
  - Number of staff who have/utilize personal digital assistants (PDAs), cell phones, laptops, and any other electronics that are owned by the nonprofit.

Vendor Information for Any Outsourced Functions

Do these vendors have business continuity plans? As a customer, you have the right to know. Ask them.

- Payroll.
- Janitorial.
- Building management.

- Clerical.
- IT and/or Web hosting.
- Other.

Vehicles

If your nonprofit owns vehicles, be sure to include information on their vehicle identification numbers (VIN), copies of the titles and registrations, and cross-references to the auto insurance policy.

Records

For the DIAD session, bring information on the location of important records (especially if the records are stored electronically), such as insurance policies, documents related to the building and furnishings, human resources, development, finance, programs (including client information), grants, contracts, and information on key equipment and supplies (including warranties).

Restricted Information

These types of information should be available only on a need-to-know basis to authorized individuals including senior management and the board's executive committee.

- Signature authority: There should be a listing of the names of the individuals who have current signatory authority.
- Account numbers for bank accounts and any other accounts at financial institutions.
- Bank codes and other security access information.

The business continuity planning document prepared in the DIAD session should also have an *executive section* that describes the *sources of funding for resumption of business operations, account numbers, and security codes.* This executive section should be distributed *only to* the executive committee of the board and to senior management. The board may also want to have emergency financial management protocols in place to trigger changes in financial operations on a limited, emergency basis. These emergency protocols need to be included in the executive section and submitted to the nonprofit's bank at the time the protocols are triggered. The bank should have a copy of the emergency financial protocols that were approved by the board. Further, there needs to be a written agreement with the bank about the way in which these protocols will be triggered. In the event of an emergency the bank needs to know who will be contacting them, how long the protocols will be in effect and the name of the individual at your nonprofit who is the authorized financial manager, i.e. CFO during the time of the crisis.

Nonprofit Operations—Basic Information

Each operational division within the nonprofit should have some basic instructions for the person who is tasked with running the division in the event of an emergency. Each division should have its own user manual that includes only that information that is necessary and sufficient. The following list of functional areas need to include all of the information that would be important for someone to know if that individual was tasked with leading the division in an emergency. For example, if a hurricane hit your city and your nonprofit's offices were severely damaged. Many of the nonprofit's departmental heads are not available because they were injured. Others in your nonprofit would be called upon to lead a department in the absence of the department head. What would they need to know to get that department up and running? As you review the sample shown for financial operations, consider what the specific functional areas in your nonprofit are. These functional areas could include:

- Administration including executive and board support.
- Human resources including volunteer administration.
- Development and fundraising.
- Programs.
- Information technology.
- Public relations.

As an example, consider the information that should be covered in describing financial operations. How would you describe your nonprofit?

Financial Operations

- Describe how payroll is prepared, or if it is outsourced, the type of information that is due to the vendor by a particular date in time.
- Describe how to prepare a bank deposit and document the deposit.
- Describe how incoming checks are processed and recorded.
- Describe the process for approving an invoice and writing a check for payment.
- Describe how check stock and the nonprofit's letterhead are secured.
- Describe the process for reimbursement of expenses originally paid by staff and/or volunteers.
- Describe the process for authorizing a merchandise order and taking delivery of the order.
- Describe the nonprofit's internal controls for financial operations.

Prepare a simple chart to organize these data for every department at your nonprofit. For example, in the nonprofit's financial operations, you might list:

Function	Primary Staff	Alternate Staff
Payroll	Mary Smith	Bob Muller
Accounts Payable	Bob Muller	Sue Nesbitt

Don't Reinvent the Wheel—Even Outdated Plans Can Be Edited

If your nonprofit has plans in place for evacuation or for business resumption, that's great. Even if the plans are out of date, they can be easily updated. It's easier and faster to edit than to create. If your nonprofit has some or all of the following materials, be sure to bring them to the session:

- Evacuation plan that provides a method to determine if all persons in the facility were evacuated.

- Evacuation plan that provides an alternative work site to resume operations if necessary.

- Emergency contact information for all staff and board members.

- Alternative e-mail addresses for all staff and board members if your nonprofit's e-mail suffers a failure.

- A system to protect paper-only records and documents in the event of a fire or water damage .

- A system to cross-train staff within operational functions.

- An alternative supply of needed items (stationary, disks, etc.) in the event that the nonprofit's offices cannot be accessed.

- List of emergency numbers (police, fire, nonprofit, etc.).

- Method to communicate with clients and/or deliver services in the event that the nonprofit's offices cannot be accessed.

- Method to contact the media in the event that the nonprofit's offices cannot be accessed.

- Instructions to staff in the event of a bomb threat.

- Instructions to staff in the event of a hazardous materials event.

- Floor plan of all floors of your nonprofit, including location of emergency exits and fire extinguishers.

- Location of all first aid kits.

One Week in Advance

- Confirm that the work groups are on track, but *DON'T CHANGE THE DIAD DATE* if they are not on track. The information that needs to be incorporated into the business continuity plan will simply be added to the day's agenda, and the session will be a bit longer. Make it clear that deliverables are due right in time for the DIAD session or a bit prior so things can be copied.

- Remind participants that they need to give family members the phone number of the receptionist on duty that day as cell phones and pagers will be banned from the session.
- Brief the facilitator on the progress so far and how the agenda for the session will be structured. Be sure to review the deliverables for the day and the session timeline to ensure that a beginning, a middle, and an end are scheduled.

The Week of the Session

- Have a walk-through meeting for the team and the facilitator at least three prior to the session to review the agenda and to ensure that the checklist for materials is complete, that there are backups for the team members, and that there are backups for the people who are tasked with bringing materials and refreshments.
- Order food and beverages for lunch and breaks.
- Brief reception staff on taking messages for the team members.
- Schedule supplies and materials to be in place in the meeting room on the day of the session. Materials needed include:
  - Flip chart with markers.
  - Laptop computer (which will be used for the slide presentation and to record the findings for the first edition of the business continuity planning plan) and printer.

    Important! Designate a "recording secretary" for the session. This individual need not be a member of the team, but could be a staff member or key volunteer. The individual should be conversant with the use of a laptop and with word processing software.
  - LCD projector.
  - Coffee, water, and/or other refreshments for team members.
  - "Perks" to be distributed at the end of the sessions.

As the preparation for the session commences, the team leader should document what is needed for the session, where supplies and refreshments were obtained, and any other information that can be saved to facilitate the setup of the next round of business continuity planning.

THE DONE IN A DAY SESSION

The day has come for the DIAD session to construct your nonprofit's business continuity plan. As with the DIAD session for risk management, take steps to ensure that the planning team is ready to begin work.

Step 1.   Before the session begins, ensure that participants are completely focused on the session. Cell phones and pagers must be *turned off*. Participants *may not take phone calls or return to their desks at any time during the DIAD session.* Emergency phone calls are to be routed to a designated receptionist.

Step 2.   Make sure there are alternates on the team in case someone is absent or called away for an emergency. The session should not be held up or adversely affected because a key player is absent.

Step 3.   The materials needed for the session include:
- Flipchart with markers.
- Laptop (which will be used for the slide presentation and to record the findings for the first edition of the business continuity planning plan) and printer.
- LCD projector.
- Water and/or other refreshments for participants.

The facilitator and the team leadership need to be committed to keeping the discussion moving along. The facilitator should advise the participants that he or she has the prerogative to intervene to redirect the conversation when a participant is either attempting to dominate or is long-winded. Keeping track of the time for each of the sections is vital to the success of the day. The times listed for each section are for illustration purposes only. You may assign any length of time to each segment. Keep in mind that the longer a session goes, the more likely it is that fatigue will impair planning progress.

DIAD Business Continuity Planning Session Agenda

[Estimated Time = 7 hours 30 minutes including break and working lunch]

Part I   Introduction to Business Continuity Planning [30 minutes]

Part II   Crisis Incident Management [90 minutes]

Break   Team members may not return to their desks during the break [15 minutes]

Part III   Essential Functions [90 minutes]

Lunch and Part IV   Business Resumption Strategies [90 minutes]

Part V   Assembling the Business Continuity Plan Using the Template [60 minutes]

Break   Team members may not return to their desks during the break [15 minutes]

Part VI   Next Steps, Deliverables, and Timetable for Update of Plan [60 minutes]

Sample Format of a DIAD Session

The facilitator and/or team leader can use this sample "script" to preside over the DIAD session.

Part I Introduction to Business Continuity Planning [30 minutes]

This slide presentation is the "executive summary" of the more extensive training for staff and volunteers that is presented in Chapter 8. The intent is to review the basic steps in business continuity planning and describe how the session will be structured. The facilitator and/or the business continuity team leader should facilitate the slide presentation.

Introduction to Business Continuity Planning

What Is Business Continuity Planning?

Business continuity planning (BCP) is the means by which a nonprofit can develop and document the policies, procedures, activities, and protocols necessary to resume essential business operations immediately following a business interruption.

What Are the Sources of Business Interruptions?
- Natural
  - Earthquake
  - Flood
  - Civil
  - Riot
  - Police action
- Person-made
  - Computer virus or worm infestation
  - Workplace violence
- Other Business Interruptions
  - Fire
  - Loss of electrical power
  - Corruption of financial or operational databases
  - Loss of major client(s) or contracts
  - Bomb threat
  - Loss of essential members of staff or executive team

What Are the Benefits of BCP?

Having an effective plan allows the nonprofit to:
- Remain a viable entity, ready to serve regardless of what happens
- Maintain the confidence and trust of clients, suppliers, staff, and other stakeholders

In the event of a natural disaster that affects the broader community, such as earthquake or fire, BCP helps the nonprofit to:
- Continue to offer products and services to clients
- Provide support to clients and staff who may be experiencing the impact of the disaster

Beginning to Plan: First Steps
- Visible commitment to BCP by top management
- Introduction of BCP concepts to staff and managers
- Visible involvement of top management
- Creation of a cross-functional team

Identify Possible Business Interruptions
- Consider both likely and unlikely interruptions
- Evaluate interruptions in terms of severity

Determine Essential Business Functions
- What nonprofit activities and functions are essential for your nonprofit?
- Who performs these activities and functions?
- Are there written protocols and procedures for these activities and functions?

Examples of Essential Functions
- Administration
- Human resources
- Payroll
- Finance
- Client service
- IT

Typical Plan Protocols
- Evacuation of staff, clients, and visitors
- Communication with stakeholders
- Public relations and media contact
- Client services
- Alternative work and service delivery sites
- Staff status, availability, and notification, including emergency contact information
- Protection of paper-only records
- Financial
  - Funds
  - Insurance coverage, claims procedures, loss documentation
  - Use of credit
  - Check writing and monitoring
  - Fund transfers and wiring
  - Security of confidential transaction and other codes

Things to Consider
- Development of remote access to data files
- Identification of resource needs for business resumption and where they can be obtained quickly
- Have staff and managers developed a personal/home plan?
- Creation of contingency plans for supplies, inventory, or other essentials

Keeping the Plan Alive
- "Desktop" simulation
- Actual simulation of a business-interruption scenario
- Employee orientation
- Ongoing practice and critique
- Continuous refinement of plan

Business Continuity Planning Template

The facilitator should walk the participants through the template outline. The template is the logical extension of the slide presentation as it represents the basic framework for the business continuity plan (see Exhibit 7.1).

Next, facilitator *describes and lists* the deliverables for the session, with emphasis on their documentation and the assignment of individual responsibility for deadlines. An important element in the deliverables is the list of the actions that will comprise "Next Steps" once the DIAD session is completed. Assign flip chart pages to capturing the ideas for "next steps."

Part II Crisis Incident Management [90 minutes]

The facilitator will ask the group to identify the potential ways in which your nonprofit's operations could be disrupted. This exercise is important but should not be belabored. The discussion for this topic should be limited to 15 minutes. The goal of the exercise is to raise team members' awareness that a business interruption can be caused by natural disasters and man-made causes, but other events as well, such as the loss of a key person. The facilitator can refer the group to the

EXHIBIT 7.1 **TABLE OF CONTENTS FOR THE BUSINESS CONTINUITY PLANNING TEMPLATE**

Incident Management
Steps to Managing the Crisis or Emergency Scenario
This section includes information from the worksheets on incident management

- Emergency scenario leadership
- Evacuation of office or other operational site
- Contact emergency personnel: fire, police, medical
- Communication among senior management, board and staff
- Media contacts [list your organization's most important media contacts]
- Emergency fundraising

Resuming Operations—Information gathered via the worksheets

- Operational priorities—what tasks must be completed every day, week, month
- Reports or other deadline items
- Materials and software needed to complete the operational priorities
- Key personnel
- IT needs
- Public sector contacts
- Private sector contacts
- Location of essential documents and files (can be hard copy or electronic)
- Vendors, contractors, and subcontractors
- Alternative sites—Information of alternative sites and basic requirements from worksheets

Strategies for Financing Business Resumption

Timetable for Updating the Business Continuity Plan

---

examples mentioned in the introductory slide presentation. The goal is to have the participants consider a wider scope of damages than just physical damage. Although damages can result from property damage, the more subtle damage through adverse publicity can be more devastating and longer in duration.

Next the facilitator will introduce the steps that the nonprofit will take in managing a crisis incident. The discussion will describe:

- *Crisis incident management leadership.* The leadership is made up of the nonprofit's team tasked with leading the organization's response to the crisis.

- *Emergency situations.* The facilitator should review the list of potential disruption scenarios that was developed in the previous exercise.

- *Evacuation planning.* The facilitator should review the nonprofit's options for evacuation of the premises.

- *Crisis communications plan.* The facilitator and the BCP team leader should review the nonprofit's crisis communication plan and/or introduce a revised plan based on the needs of the current situation.

- *Emergency fundraising.* The facilitator and the BCP team leader should review the nonprofit's emergency plan and/or introduce a revised plan based on the needs of the current situation.

- *Determining extent of damage.* The BCP planning team should be briefed on methods used for assessing extent of physical damage and of institutional damage, such as adverse publicity.

- *Nonprofit's expectations of staff and volunteers.* The BCP planning team should identify key expectations of staff and volunteers during a crisis scenario, such as staying in contact with the nonprofit, working hours or shifts that are not their normal workday, substituting in a department other than their own, and other complementary alternatives.

Break [15 minutes]
Part III Essential Functions [90 minutes]
In this segment, the facilitator asks the team to present the essential functions for each of the nonprofit's divisions. The purpose of this exercise is twofold: 1) Identifying your nonprofit's most important operational functions. Each of the divisions in your nonprofit has functions

that are essential to the resumption of business; 2) Identifying the steps or actions that need to be taken to re-start these essential functions.

- Assume that your nonprofit's offices are destroyed and that you must resume operations in an alternative location. List the most important functions for each of your nonprofit's divisions.

- Once you have identified these important functions, consider what someone would need to know to resume the operations. Remember, not all department heads will be available after an emergency. The person who takes over for the departmental head will need to know where the important files, contact information, or other data are located and how to access this information if it is password protected. What steps must be taken to complete each task?

The team can construct a chart (see Exhibit 7.2) that shows the primary staff assigned to each functions and the name of the staff member who has been (or will be) trained to step in if the primary staffer is not available.

For example, in the nonprofit's financial operations:

Function	Primary Staff	Alternate Staff
Payroll	Mary Smith	Bob Muller
Accounts Payable	Bob Muller	Sue Nesbitt

EXHIBIT 7.2   DEPTH OF STAFFING

Critical Function	Primary Staff	Alternate Staff

EXHIBIT 7.3	RESUMING OPERATIONS CRITICAL FUNCTIONS RESUMED BY PRIORITY

Critical Function	Strategy for Resuming Operation ASAP

For each of the major functions that the team has identified, begin to list the ways in which this function can be restored to operation as soon as possible if your nonprofit's office is destroyed or cannot be accessed (see Exhibit 7.3). The strategies listed in the table below are for illustration only. Each function should have several strategies to address the immediate needs of the department.

Critical Function	Strategy for Resuming Operation ASAP
Human Resources	Use staff availability checklist to assign staff to shifts.
Finance	Arrange for payroll data to be delivered to vendor for direct deposits.
Administration	Contact executive committee of board for authorization to trigger emergency financial administration protocols.

Lunch and Part IV Business Resumption Strategies [90 minutes]

The discussion during the working lunch should focus on how your nonprofit might respond to each of the next issues to resume operations effectively. The facilitator should appoint someone to either take notes or write the main ideas on a flip chart for later transcription and discussion.

- Ensuring that people are safe—staff and volunteers. Does everyone know what is expected of them? Do they have the equipment and resources to work from home? Can they access their files from home? How do they communicate with their supervisors?

- Identifying what the nonprofit needs in terms of resources and equipment for business resumption and where the resources and equipment can be obtained quickly. What will your nonprofit need to resume operations? Where can you obtain these supplies if your primary vendors are affected by the emergency? Do you have a list of back-up vendors?

- Ensuring that financial resources are in place to resume financial operations even at a different location. What information and resources will your plan need to include to ensure that your nonprofit can pay its bills and accept emergency donations?

- How might your nonprofit resume operations even if the business interruption is at a neighboring building or a street adjacent to your nonprofit's offices? Does your nonprofit have an alternative site for its operations?

- Are your electronic files, databases, e-mail, and software that are currently housed on your computers backed up and stored offsite? How often? Can these files, software, and databases be accessed easily? Has the backup been tested to see if it works?

- Have staff and managers developed a personal/home plan?

Part V Assembling the Business Continuity Plan
[60 minutes]
The facilitator then begins the process of integrating all of the material prepared in the weeks prior to the DIAD session with the corresponding section of the template.

Crisis Incident Management
This section would include:

- Evacuation plan that provides a method to determine if all persons in the facility were evacuated

- Emergency contact information for all staff and board members
- Alternative e-mail addresses for all staff and board members if your nonprofit's e-mail suffers a failure
- A system to protect paper-only records and documents in the event of a fire or water damage
- List of emergency numbers (police, fire, nonprofit, etc.)
- Method to communicate with clients and/or deliver services in the event that the nonprofit's offices cannot be accessed
- Crisis communication plan
- Emergency fundraising plan

Business Resumption

This section would include:

- Essential functions and depth of staffing
- Staff and board contact list
- Vendor contact list
- Other key contacts, such as utilities and public agencies
- Equipment and supplies needed to resume operations
- IT infrastructure
- Alternative work site to resume operations if necessary
- A system to cross-train staff within operational functions
- An alternative supply of needed items (stationery, disks, etc.) in the event that the nonprofit's offices cannot be accessed
- *For Executive Edition of business continuity plan only:* Business resumption financing strategies and bank accounts/codes
  - Insurance
  - Line of credit
  - Other sources of credit or funding

The information needs to be transcribed onto the template. The facilitator should ensure that all of the sections of the template are completed in a manner that meets the needs of the nonprofit.

Break [15 minutes]
Part VI Next Steps, Deliverables, and Timetable for
Update of Plan [60 minutes]
The remainder of the session should focus on the next steps that were identified from the working lunch and throughout the session. The list of next steps should be transformed into action steps with specific deliverables, deadlines, and individuals named to be responsible for them.

The BCP team leader should thank the team and the facilitator for their hard work, distribute perks, and adjourn the session.

SUMMARY

The business continuity plan has two major components: crisis incident management and business resumption. As your nonprofit's business continuity plan develops, it is important for the planning team to design strategies to move the organization from managing the crisis incident to resuming operations. The more quickly that takes place, the faster the critical functions will be restored. Rapid access to electronic files, documents, databases, and software is the key, as is a solid plan for alternative sources of equipment and supplies.

The staff and volunteers of your nonprofit will become proficient in dealing with emergency situations and subsequent business resumption only through routine practice at emergency evacuation and business resumption scenarios. Chapter 8 describes methods for offering these types of exercises.

PART THREE

Adding Value to Risk Management and Business Continuity Planning

Training in Risk Management and Business Contingency Planning for Staff and Volunteers

LEVERAGING TRAINING FOR MAXIMUM RESULTS

Your team has worked hard to prepare materials and develop a risk management and/or business continuity plan. You know that unless everyone in the organization participates in the execution of the plan, it won't work. How do you get everyone on the same page? How do you explain what the plans are about and how these plans are intended to facilitate real and lasting change?

The answer to these questions lies in the design of a really good training curriculum for your staff and volunteers. The plan should, first and foremost, present the concepts clearly and illustrate what best practices look like. The risk management and/or business continuity plan should reinforce the nonprofit's values and mission. The tone and content of the plan needs to resonate with staff and volunteers—they need to understand how the training affects what they do and how they do it. Even more compelling, the training should describe new behaviors and expectations and explain *why* these changes are essential to the well-being of the organization and its continued viability.

The curriculum should also describe how the whole organization will integrate these new concepts and what the staff and volunteers can expect to see in operational and procedural changes. The training needs to be clear on what everyone is expected to do differently. Of particular importance is the description of the ways in which the board and senior management have adopted the new practices.

The training should describe the need for ongoing training and what the staff and volunteers can expect in the way of regularly scheduled briefings or exercises. An important element in launching the initial and recurring training is to offer an opportunity for staff and volunteers to contribute to the experience, in other words, identify areas that the nonprofit should consider in terms of risk management planning, crisis incident management, or business continuity. The more fully engaged staff and volunteers are in the changes, the more readily they will adopt those changes.

DESIGNING A CURRICULUM THAT WORKS

The training agenda need not be complex. Effective training uses pedagogical methods that are appropriate to adult learners and employs a variety of methods, such as in-service sessions, that convey the concepts and methods in a manner specific to the delivery of services. Small group training can foster a team approach while trainees learn about risk management and/or business continuity planning. An important companion piece to training is practical application, which can come in the form of desktop exercises and disaster drills. Consider how specific types of training can facilitate implementation of risk management or business continuity best practices. Develop a chart that identifies risk areas or policies that should be reviewed and develop training to address these issues. Exhibit 8.1 presents a sample agenda.

The purpose of the agenda is to track the risk management training that takes place in each department. Once the introductory risk

| EXHIBIT 8.1 | RISK MANAGEMENT TRAINING AGENDA | | |

Department	Intro Risk Management Training	Policy Review?	Other Risk Areas

management training is presented, the department can then review its policies to identify any areas that need written policies or identify any other risk issues in the department's operations that need attention.

For larger organizations, the training can be delivered utilizing technology, such as the intranet or Web-based training. Electronic storage, such as Web links or CDs, can be utilized to store training materials and other resources for easy and immediate access.

The most carefully designed training is not successful if no one learns how to apply the new concepts and practices. Any training curriculum should include simple assessment techniques and methods to evaluate the success of the training. Some easy-to-apply methods are:

- *"Before" and "after" quizzes to test skills.* Participants can be given a short quiz on risk management and/or business continuity planning before the session and another one immediately following the session. Give a small prize for "most improved" results.

- *Practical demonstration of skills.* Staff and volunteers can illustrate that they understand the concepts and practices by their performance in desktop exercises, disaster drills, or risk identification.

- *Demonstration that concepts and best practices have been integrated into everyday work activities.* This is the most important way in which your nonprofit can observe success in training.

Although no one can predict when an emergency will occur or its impact, staff and volunteers will have a better chance of surviving an emergency if they are confident about what to do and that they have the ability to do what is needed in a crisis.

SAMPLE TRAINING AGENDAS AND CURRICULA

Risk Management Training

The introductory risk management training should be approximately 45 minutes in length. The idea is to introduce the concepts and practices of risk management along with the structure of the risk management plan that the nonprofit has adopted. If appropriate, the entire risk management plan could be disseminated, but the executive summary of the plan could also suffice. The most important deliverable from the session is the introduction of new methods and practices to everyday operations.

Sample Outline of an Introductory Training Session on Risk Management

Session Objectives
- Define risk management and identify risk management tools.
- Examine how risk management activities can be incorporated into everyday work activities.
- Discuss what you can do to keep [the name of your nonprofit] safe.

What Is Risk Management?
- Risk management is the means by which a nonprofit can identify, assess, and control risks that may be present within the organization. Risk management is not just about

identifying risks; it is about learning to work safely, to comply with policies and procedures that strengthen internal controls, and to help your nonprofit maintain its good name and reputation.

How Does Risk Management Work?
There are three basic activities in risk management:
  1. *Risk assessment.* This is the process of evaluating potential for accidents, injuries, insurance claims, or adverse publicity. Risks areas are prioritized, and possible risk treatment approaches are considered.
  2. *Implementation of risk management activities.* In implementation, action steps are taken to treat identified risks. Decisions are made on how to deal with the risks that were identified in the risk assessment. Once a decision is made on how to deal with the risk, action steps are assigned to ensure that the risk treatment is carried out and that the metrics are in place to determine if the treatment was effective. These metrics can include a comparison of injuries and accidents, or the number of complaints made about creaky stairs, etc.
  3. *Risk management administration and monitoring.* This step ensures that the actions taken in the risk management activities are reviewed to determine effectiveness and to establish a framework for the next round of risk assessment.

Four Primary Ways to Deal with Risks
A risk strategy, however, can be a blend of two or more of these techniques. Remember, you can't eliminate risk altogether—it's a part of life!
  1. *Avoidance.* Just say "no" and stop doing the activity. This is usually not feasible in a nonprofit setting as the activity may be an important program.
  2. *Retention.* Risk retention acknowledges that a risk exists. To deal with it, the nonprofit sets up a fund to pay for losses.

This option isn't always feasible, but other variations on it, such as raising insurance deductibles, can be helpful.

3. *Modification.* Modification is a technique that changes the dynamics around a risk. Policies and procedures are put in place to reduce the potential for an accident or loss. The idea is to change frequency and severity of loss.

4. *Transfer.* Risk transfer means that the nonprofit transfers risk to a third party, such as an insurance company, for a fee. Risk can also be transferred in contract language, such as a hold harmless clause.

How Does Risk Avoidance Work at Your Nonprofit?
The risk management committee considered possible risks in these four areas of the organization:

1. Board
2. Staff and Volunteers
3. Operations
4. Relations with the public

The committee determined what risk areas needed to be addressed during this round of risk management training and established strategies to deal with the risks. [If your nonprofit provides a summary of the risk management plan, this section would include a section on key areas of risk management attention.] The results are contained in the handout distributed to session participants (which could be the full report or an executive summary).

- *Describe highlights of the findings.* Explain what types of risks were identified and what is being done to mitigate the risks.
- *Describe new expectations for staff and volunteers.* Explain that risk management is not a fad. It is a management tool that holds great benefit for the nonprofit, but it won't work unless everyone fully participates.

Risk management activities are ongoing - The committee will reconvene in (give the time frame i.e. 3 months, 6 months) to begin the process again.

How You Can Help: Your Role in Risk Management

In this part of the training, you can present the ways in which staff and volunteers are expected to help integrate risk management practices into their daily work. Give specific recommendations for changes in either workplace performance or behavior.

Conclude the session by providing the participants with specific recommendations for new behaviors or procedures that address the primary risk areas. Thank everyone for attending and adjourn.

BUSINESS CONTINUITY TRAINING

The introductory training on business continuity planning is especially important because it serves as the gateway to an array of training exercises that relate to various aspects of crisis incident management and business resumption. Staff and volunteers who attend the introductory training will also be expected to participate in emergency evacuation exercises, crisis communication exercises, and desktop exercises. The overall objective of this type of training is to facilitate a greater level of self-efficacy, which, in turn, will improve staff and volunteer performance in an emergency and in subsequent business resumption.

Sample Outline of an Introductory Training Session on Business Continuity Planning

What Is Business Continuity Planning?
Business Continuity Planning (BCP) is the means by which a nonprofit can develop and document the policies, procedures, activities, and protocols necessary to resume essential business operations immediately following a business interruption.

What Are the Sources of Business Interruptions?
- Natural
  - Earthquake
  - Flood
- Civil
  - Riot
  - Police action

- Person-made
  - Computer virus or worm infestation
  - Workplace violence
- Other business interruptions
  - Fire
  - Loss of electrical power
  - Corruption of financial or operational databases
  - Loss of major client(s) or contracts
  - Bomb threat
  - Loss of essential members of staff or executive team

What Are the Benefits of BCP?

Having an effective plan allows the nonprofit to:

- Remain a viable entity, ready to serve regardless of what happens
- Maintain the confidence and trust of clients, suppliers, staff, and other stakeholders
- Continue to offer products and services to clients and provide support to clients and staff who may be experiencing the impact of the disaster, in the event of a natural disaster that affects the broader community

There Has Been a Crisis Incident at Your Nonprofit. What Should You Do?

Evacuation Procedures

- Identify stairways, doors, or other emergency exits. [Identify these for your nonprofit.]
- Specify a location where all staff, volunteers, clients, and visitors are to meet so that management team can do a head count. [Identify a primary meeting place and an alternate meeting place for your nonprofit's staff and volunteers.]
- Establish protocols to assist police, firefighters, and other emergency personnel, such as affixing special logos to the door of an office occupied by an individual with a vision or mobility impairment.

In the event of a fire:

Evacuate the building and relocate through stairwells, *not elevators,* to the ground floor. If your building has an intercom system, be sure that the emergency announcement can be heard on all floors and in all offices.

- Alert everyone and ask them to remain calm but move quickly. In an emergency, every moment counts. The calmer that the staff, volunteers, and visitors remain, the faster they can evacuate the building.
- Listen for instructions and report to the designated emergency exits. Staff and volunteers should be trained ahead of any crisis situation to listen for instructions and know where the nearest emergency exit is. Once out of the buildings, staff and volunteers should know that they are prohibited from returning to the building until the "all clear" signal is given.
- Everybody has to be accounted for before anyone— member of staff, volunteers, visitors, or whomever—is permitted to go home. The crisis management team must have a list of individuals who have been accounted for, a list of those who were not in the building that day, and a list of those who have not been accounted for. The team should give this list to the fire captain so that emergency responders will have an idea of how many people may still be in the building. *Staff and volunteers should understand that full cooperation in terms of census-taking is mandatory and that failure to cooperate may result in disciplinary action.*
- Go to the emergency meeting place. Actually, there should be *two* emergency meeting places. If, for some reason, it is not safe to congregate at the primary meeting place, everyone needs to know where the alternative meeting place is. As part of the disaster drills, staff and volunteers should occasionally be directed to meet at the alternative meeting place.

- Keep clear of the building to avoid falling debris. Once staff and volunteers have assembled and are accounted for, it is important that they understand to keep a safe distance from the building and *stay out of the way of emergency responders.*

Location of First Aid and Emergency Supplies

Your nonprofit should have at least one first aid kit and emergency supplies, such as flashlights and batteries. All staff and volunteers should know where these items are located.

- First aid kits contain: rubbing alcohol, hydrogen peroxide, anesthetic antiseptic ointment, gauze pads, cloth tape, Band-Aids, bandages, cold pack, scissors, tweezers, and Tylenol.
- The location of any emergency food supplies and water located
- Flashlights should be located at each workstation.
- Heavy-duty gloves for debris removal located at
- Portable radios and batteries Contact information (such as pager or cell phone) of individuals who will be certified in first aid and/or CPR training.

In case of a power outage:

If you are in the elevator at the time of a power outage, remain calm and follow these instructions:

- Push the button to sound the buzzer alarm in the elevator.
- Open the phone box and follow instructions.
  - The plan should give the location of emergency phones, flashlights, portable radios, and batteries and their features.

Ensure that an alarm has been sounded and that the staff, volunteers, and clients know that they must evacuate the building. Follow the evacuation plan and exit the building immediately.

Your Nonprofit's Plan

In this section describe your nonprofit's strategies for:

- Evacuation of staff and volunteers, clients, and visitors
- Communication with stakeholders
- Public relations and media contact
- Client services
- Alternative work and service delivery sites
- Staff status, availability, and notification, including emergency contact information
- Protection of paper-only records
- Strategies for resuming operations

How You Can Help: Your Role in Crisis Incident Management and Business Resumption
This section of the training will focus on what is expected of staff and volunteers in the event of an emergency and in the subsequent business resumption component.

Your Role in Preserving the Good Name and Reputation of the Nonprofit
Refer all media inquiries to the selected spokesperson. This individual has the most accurate information and is trained to deal with the media. The nonprofit's good name hinges on its professionalism, particularly during a crisis or emergency. Politely decline to make any comment or personal response to a reporter, as you may not have all of the facts. It is important that you support your nonprofit by making sure that the media is directed to the spokesperson.

Training Staff on Their Role in Helping the Nonprofit Resume Operations
- Staff should be ready to complete a staff availability checklist. Show the staff a sample of a completed form in Exhibit 8.2.

Staff should also understand that in the event of an emergency their normal work routine will be changed and might not resume for a significant length of time.
- In the event of an emergency, you may be asked to work hours that are different from your normal hours, in a

EXHIBIT 8.2   SAMPLE STAFF AVAILABILITY CHECKLIST FOR MORNINGSIDE SOCIAL SERVICES IN THE AFTERMATH OF A HURRICANE

Staff Member Name: <u>Susan Smith</u>

Department: <u>Development and Fundraising</u>

Active Phone Number: <u>555-1222</u>

Present Residence Address: <u>1234 Sunnyside Lane</u>

Home E-mail: <u>Susie@familyemail.com</u>

Any injuries to staff member?   ☐ yes   ☒ no

If yes, nature of injury

_____

Any injuries to family member?   ☒ yes   ☐ no

If yes, nature of injury: <u>Husband broke his arm.</u>

Any serious damage to staff member's property?   ☒ yes   ☐ no

If yes, nature of injury: <u>Substantial damage to roof of house—fallen trees on the property.</u>

Best times for this staff person to work his or her shift:

<u>Mornings from 9AM—1PM</u>

Any time this staff person could not work: ☒ yes   ☐ no

If yes, specify why? <u>Afternoons. Need to supervise contractors at home.</u>

Transportation: Does this person have transportation?   ☒ yes   ☐ no

Can this person assist others in getting to work?   ☒ yes   ☐ no

_____

Does the staff member need any assistance?   ☒ yes   ☐ no

If yes, specify: <u>I'd like assistance in dealing with my health insurance provider.</u>

different location from your current workplace, and doing a job that may be different from your normal position.
- You will need to keep in contact with your supervisor or the designated crisis management team member.
- You may need to assist your colleagues in getting to work or in performing tasks.

Discuss the Content of the Nonprofit's Business Continuity Plan and the Staff Role in Business Resumption
In the DIAD session, the first draft of the business continuity plan was prepared. As part of the session, a list of "next steps" was drafted to identify the type of information that would be necessary to round out the plan and to facilitate the resumption of operations. In the staff training, present the list of next steps to be completed in 90 days and 180 days that was drafted at the DIAD session. Future steps should include:
- Arranging to have each division within the nonprofit prepare a document that outlines what would need to be done to resume operations in the division. Each division's document is essentially a "users' manual" to jump-start the division.
- Testing out each of the division's resumption plans. Explain that during an upcoming desktop exercise, a designated person (from outside the division) will be given the document on how to jump-start the division operations. Based on the information in this document, the person will be expected to take steps to resume operations in that division. The person may have a difficult time if the document is not clear and informative. More importantly, the division's operations will not be resumed.
- Editing and revising the division's resumption plan to ensure that someone outside the division can resume operations using the plan.

Keeping the Plan Alive
Describe the ways that your nonprofit plans to conduct emergency drills and desktop exercises.

- Explain why your nonprofit is committed to emergency preparation.
- Explain what your nonprofit expects from staff and volunteers. It is important to be straightforward about expectations, particularly in terms of having to work different hours than their normal workdays and perhaps in different locations.
- Explain how this training and the BCP will help your nonprofit in the event of real emergency.

Summarize the key points of the training and describe the next steps. Thank everyone for attending and adjourn.

HANDS-ON TRAINING EXERCISES

Your nonprofit has a risk management and/or business continuity plan and you've trained your staff. Now what? To ensure that the knowledge from this planning changes behavior in your nonprofit, it is essential that this planning is fully integrated into your nonprofit's organizational culture by means of routinely scheduled exercises. As was illustrated in the story about the Morgan Stanley staff on September 11, 2001, the routine practice of having emergency evacuation drills saved lives. Helping staff learn to be confident in emergency situations is more than just a fire drill. Communicating clear behavioral and performance expectations to staff is particularly important. Explain to staff what their obligations are as well as what they can expect from the management of the nonprofit. Emphasize that normal work hours and location of the nonprofit's offices may have to change.

Nature and Use of Emergency Preparedness Exercises

Adult learners of all ages respond well to experiential learning. The introductory training sessions described in this chapter present the framework for understanding risk management and business continuity planning. The next step is for staff and volunteers to gain enough "experience" through emergency exercises that they understand what is expected of them in an emergency. Staff need to also understand that the actions that may have to take place to resume operations and what their role(s) might be in helping the nonprofit resume operations. Depending on the type of emergency, staff may be asked to take on more than one job in the organization. If the emergency is a hurricane or earthquake, their colleagues might be injured or otherwise not available to come into work. The more staff have practiced emergency exercises and business resumption simulations, the better prepared they will be for the real thing.

Practice, Practice, Practice

The more often a behavior is reinforced, the less likely the individual will forget what is expected or, worse yet, panic when a real emergency arises. It is important that *everyone present in the nonprofit office or facility participates* in these emergency exercises. That was the rule at Morgan Stanley during the fire drills in the years after the first terrorist attack. *Everyone* was required to leave by the nearest stairwell when the alarm sounded.

How to Set Up and Conduct Emergency Evacuation Exercises for Different Scenarios

The scenarios for emergency evacuation drills should vary. Fire drills are the most common, but also include a scenario that is a power outage. The incidence of workplace violence is a sad commentary on today's business environment. Sometimes the violence is directly related to the work environment or a human resources HR decision, but sometimes it is a spillover of domestic violence. Exercises relating to workplace violence need to be a part of your nonprofit's array of practical training.

An easy way to design an emergency evacuation exercise is to begin with the material that you presented as part of the introductory training on business continuity planning. Review the evacuation procedures for your nonprofit's facility. Identify stairways, doors, or other emergency exits. Are floor plans posted in strategic areas around the building? Does your building have illuminated exit signs near stairways? If not, it is important that you take the time to ensure that all staff and volunteers know the location of all of the stairs leading out of the building.

Once the staff and volunteers—and visitors—are out of the building, everyone must know where they are to meet so that someone on the management team can do a head count. Make sure that staff members know who is taking the head count and who is the backup person for this function. Having an alternate meeting place for your nonprofit's staff, volunteers, and visitors to gather is equally important. The person designated to take the head count needs to report the results to the emergency responders and tell them the names and possible locations of individuals who are not present and whether these individuals have physical impairments.

Fire Drills

Before your nonprofit begins or resumes fire drills, take the time to train staff and volunteers about "best practices" that can save their lives. These best practices were introduced during the initial BCP training, but it is important to reinforce these practices as often as you can. There are two very important protocols in emergency evacuation.

1.   If you are in an office with the door closed and the fire alarm sounds, do not open the door until you have put the palm of your hand on the door to feel if there is heat. If the door feels hot, do not open it.

2.   Evacuate the building and relocate through stairwells, not elevators, to the ground floor. If your building has an intercom system, be sure that the emergency announcement can be heard on all floors and in all offices.

As part of the training, help staff and volunteers create a buddy system. The more that staff and volunteers can simulate a real event, the better the quality of the learning. For all of the fire drills, have staff ensure that their buddy is accounted for. Doing this is important in ensuring that an accurate head count can take place once everyone is evacuated. If your nonprofit has staff or volunteers who are mobility impaired, sight impaired, or hearing impaired, the drills are a good opportunity to determine the type of special attention and steps that need to be taken.

Teach staff and volunteers to listen for instructions and report to the designated emergency exits. Staff and volunteers should be trained ahead of any crisis situation to follow instructions, particularly if one of the emergency exits is not safe, or if the alternative meeting place is to be used for this scenario. Once out of the buildings, staff and volunteers should know that they are prohibited from returning to the building until the "all clear" signal is given—even during a drill. Drills should also include a formal accounting of all individuals, including those who were not in the building that day and those who have not been accounted for. *Staff and volunteers should understand that this is not the time for challenging the rules and that failure to cooperate may result in disciplinary action—even during a drill.*

Another important point in the pre-exercise briefing is the expectations of staff and volunteers once they have exited the building. They need to keep clear of the building to avoid falling debris. Once people have assembled and are accounted for, it is important that they understand to keep a safe distance from the building and *stay out of the way of emergency responders.* These behaviors need to be included as part of the drill.

Power Outage Drill

Although power outages may be relatively rare, it is important to brief staff on what to do if one occurs. Being caught in an elevator can be a frightening experience. Help staff and volunteers learn how to cope with this type of an emergency by telling them that if they are in the elevator at the time of a power outage, they should remain calm and follow these instructions:

1. Push the button to sound the buzzer alarm in the elevator.

2. Open the phone box and follow instructions.

3. If they have a cell phone, call the nonprofit's main desk or security for the building. Be sure that all staff and volunteers have the phone numbers for these emergency contacts and encourage them to put these numbers in their cell phone's memory.

Make sure all staff and volunteers know the location of emergency phones, flashlights, portable radios, and batteries: As part of their emergency preparedness training, staff should know the various locations of and features of all emergency equipment that the nonprofit has on the premises.

If possible, sound the alarm to advise staff to evacuate the building. Follow the evacuation plan and exit the building immediately. *Call 911 once you have exited the building.*

Workplace Violence Drill

Evacuation exercises that center around workplace violence scenarios need to be offered as regularly as are fire drills. Unfortunately, in today's society, violence takes place more and more often in a work location. The root of the violence can be the workplace or the home. Innocent people often lose their lives at the hand of someone with a deadly weapon. No one can predict this behavior, although there are often warning signs. Your nonprofit needs to be prepared and to have a plan that will alert staff and volunteers to evacuate without further compromising the safety of the individuals who are confronting the violent person.

Many nonprofits have a telephone system with an intercom feature. People can be paged, and everyone hears the page. If your nonprofit has this type of intercom, the receptionist can "page" a fictitious employee, such as Betty Jones; this is the code message for everyone to evacuate the building. If this type of a signal is sounded, staff and volunteers will have to evacuate from exits other than ones by the front desk. If an intercom is not available, a buzzer should be located underneath the reception desk that rings in several key offices and signal that reception staff are in trouble and need help. Your crisis incident management team needs to consider carefully the methods that would be right for your nonprofit and ensure that all staff and volunteers know how to respond in an emergency.

Sample Desktop Exercises

Desktop exercises are useful in integrating best practices and new behaviors into everyday operations because these time-limited scenarios illustrate the impact of a crisis on nonprofit's operations. Further, these exercises are useful in conveying behavioral and performance expectations.

How to Set Up and Conduct a Desktop Exercise

Before you begin the desktop exercise, you need to determine what measures of success will be applied. Do you want to see how well staff members and volunteers rise to the task of resuming operations? Do you want to have them prepare an action agenda for the two or three days following the event? Do you want to see how well one work group supports another? Participants need to know what is expected of them and what deliverables should come from the session. They also need to know the exercise will take *X* number of minutes and that they will be expected to work in groups, report back, and so on. They will be required to remain in the conference room or wherever the desktop exercise takes place.

Staff and volunteers participating in the desktop exercise will need to focus their attention entirely on the exercise and follow the instructions carefully.

Step 1. Read the scenario.

Step 2. Read the task list and determine which tasks apply to your department. Determine if other departments are involved in providing data or assistance that is needed to complete these tasks.

Step 3. Prioritize the projects that you are currently working on and the tasks from Step 2 that apply to you. Develop an action agenda containing the list of tasks and projects that are to be completed in the next two to three days.

Step 4. Develop a departmental strategy (in bullet points) that will describe how you will complete the "to do" list from Step 3. Include what you will need to do to fully resume operations within your department and what assistance you will need from other departments.

Step 5. The actual scenario that you design for your nonprofit should include these elements:

- A situation should be clearly an emergency or a crisis, such as a fire, earthquake, hurricane, loss of a key member of the staff, or some other situation that cannot be ignored.
- The situation should also have significant media interest. You must take steps to trigger the crisis communication plan.
- The situation might also include the potential for having to relocate to another office at least temporarily. For example, perhaps water has soaked your computers, files, and other office materials. The phones are not working .The building inspector has red-tagged your building until the two feet of water on the main floor can be drained and the sprinkler system restored.

The sample scenarios that follow are designed to help your team conduct effective desktop exercises. *Be sure to create scenarios that accurately reflect your nonprofit's profile, region, and a realistic emergency.* These exercises become more effective when staff and volunteers are asked to develop strategies that deal with increasingly difficult situations. The more often staff and volunteers are asked to deal with very dire situations, the better prepared they become to deal with a wide range of interruptions. Practice does make perfect and can be instrumental in helping staff and volunteers improve their confidence in dealing with emergency situations.

Sample Emergency Scenario During Business Hours

It is 2 P.M. on a Wednesday. The fire alarm sounds although there is no evidence of smoke or fire. The executive director is in the boardroom meeting with a major donor. The staff and volunteers are in the training room for an in-service. A consultant who is mobility impaired is working in an office at the back of your floor. Describe how you evacuate the building and ensure that everyone—staff, volunteers, and visitors—is out of the offices and present at the designated meeting place.

Sample Emergency Scenario After Business Hours

It is 8 P.M. on a Saturday. A fire has started on the seventh floor of the building housing the ABC Agency. By the time the firefighters arrive, the entire seventh floor is engulfed. Sprinklers throughout the building have been activated, and there is approximately three feet of standing water on each floor. The building has been red-tagged because the firefighters have determined that the flooring on the seventh floor has been seriously compromised. In several places it has crashed into the ABC offices below. Wiring and telecommunications infrastructure have been seriously damaged. Building inspectors believe that the building will remain red-tagged for at least six weeks.

If you were the executive director of the ABC Agency, what would you do? How would you ensure that your board knew what happened and that your staff knew what to do on Monday morning?

Sample Emergency Scenario: Two Locations
It is 1:30 P.M. on a sunny Friday, February 13. A police chase is taking place on Union Street. The suspect's car is traveling north at a high rate of speed. The car makes a sharp right turn on Sutter. As it is entering the intersection of Sutter and Scott, a tire on the car blows and the vehicle veers wildly across Scott Street, hitting a parked car and crashing into the administrative office of the Sunnyside Social Services Agency. There is a staff meeting going on, so no staffers are in the office, but the force of the crash causes the car's fuel tank to burst into flames, and within seconds the entire office space is on fire. The smoke detectors and sprinkler systems respond. The police car that was chasing the suspect vehicle has called in the fire to the fire department, and two engines are on the way. George Lee, reporter from the local TV station, was also riding in the police car as part of his ongoing series on police activities. It is unknown how many staffers are in their offices. Because of the fire, the front door is not available as an exit. Smoke is beginning to fill the main floor, and water is pouring from the sprinkler system. Fire trucks have arrived, and firefighters are entering the building.

Across town at Sunnyside's newest collaborative partner, the Fairview Independent Living Center, a staff member's lunch was cooking on the stove in the kitchen on the third floor of the main building. The grease in the frying pan caught fire and the terrified staff member fled the kitchen. As the flames began to roar, the smoke alarm sounded, sending four residents who were in the building out onto the street. The third-floor kitchen is now engulfed in flames, and the smoke has become even more toxic as the furnishings in the kitchen burn. The apartment of Mr. Smith, a mobility-impaired resident, is on the third floor, next to the kitchen on fire. Mr. Smith uses two canes. As the frightened residents gather on the sidewalk in front of the main building, no one has seen Mr. Smith. The fire engines have arrived, and firefighters are beginning to enter the building. Coincidentally, the "I–Team" from Channel 7 is in the neighborhood; they were doing research on a story involving a nearby hospital. The reporters see the fire engines approaching Fairview apartments and follow the emergency personnel. Fred Noyes, reporter for Channel 7, has his cameraman with him as they begin to interview the terrified families.

How Is the Success of Emergency Preparedness and Desktop Exercises Measured?

The success of a desktop exercise is directly related to the objectives and deliverables that you present prior to the start of the exercise. Some critical areas in developing a solid approach to crisis management and business resumption include:

- *Ability to follow instructions.* In order to evacuate a building safely or work collaboratively to resume business operations, staff and volunteers need to demonstrate a focused ability to follow instructions. A crisis scenario is not the time for consensus-building, even though the nonprofit's organizational culture may generally turn to this type of management style. Your team needs to be very clear—even blunt if necessary—about the obligation of everyone to do as they are told in an emergency. If this issue appears to be problematic in evacuation exercises, your team will need to increase the frequency and add variety to the exercises until everyone demonstrates that he or she can follow instructions. Individuals who demonstrate a consistent unwillingness or refusal to comply need to be counseled or disciplined. The nonprofit cannot afford to have to deal with "free thinkers" during an emergency.

- *Depth of staffing.* The term "depth of staffing" addresses the ability of staff members and volunteers to take on assignments in departments or to complete assignments different from their normal work routine. The adaptability of staff and volunteers in terms of stepping into new roles and assignments can be crucial in dealing effectively with a crisis scenario and ultimately resuming operations.

- *A business continuity plan.* Every nonprofit needs a document that contains information that is necessary and sufficient to address critical needs in the first 48 hours. Today's technology, including personal digital assistants (PDAs) such as PalmPilots and Black-Berries, contains sufficient memory space to house such documents. Members of the crisis management team should have the document housed on their PDAs and have important numbers logged onto their cell phone's directory.

- *Level of organizational efficacy.* As staff and volunteers routinely participate in desktop exercises that center around scenarios that portray the destruction of the office, they should begin to see that, despite such a dire set of circumstances, the nonprofit can continue to exist, weather the immediate crisis, and ultimately resume operations. The underlying message of the desktop exercises is that the nonprofit is *committed* to doing what is necessary to remain a viable organization positioned to serve its clients and the community.

Document results from each desktop exercise and evaluate individual performance. Compare the results after three desktop exercises to see the performance of staff members and volunteers has improved. If it has not, add in-service sessions that address the problematic issues and, if necessary, take specific corrective actions to ensure compliance.

SUMMARY

These exercises aren't just games. The responses and performance of staff and volunteers in these exercises can serve as evaluative tools for your nonprofit's risk management and business continuity plans. Before your team presents any training or practical exercises, it is important for you to set goals and objectives in terms of the skills that the staff and volunteers are expected to acquire and the performance levels desired. Clarity of expectations and clear-cut directions are essential in making the training and the exercises worthwhile. At first your team will need to run exercises on what would seem to be a never-ending basis. Remember the dividends that routine fire drills paid for the Morgan Stanley staff on that sunny September morning in 2001.

CHAPTER 9

The ROI of Risk Management and Business Continuity Planning

The only things that evolve by themselves in an organization are disorder, friction and malperformance.

—Peter Drucker

LEVERAGING RISK MANAGEMENT AND BUSINESS CONTINUITY PLANNING FOR GREATER EFFECTIVENESS

Risk management and business continuity planning pay dividends even if an accident, loss, or crisis never occurs. The return on investment (ROI) for your nonprofit's time and effort include:

- *Insurance.* Risk management and business continuity planning are important activities to demonstrate your nonprofit's commitment to being a full partner with your insurance professional and the insurance company. Producing risk management and business continuity plans confirms your nonprofit's commitment to solid management practices and may serve to provide greater access to insurance products at possibly more competitive rates.

- *Banks and financial institutions.* Banks and other financial institutions want to feel confident in a client before they are willing to offer a loan or line of credit. Your nonprofit's risk management and business continuity plans are means by which you can demonstrate to your banker or other financial professional that your nonprofit is a good lending risk. Generally interest rates are predicated on the level of risk that the institution perceives a customer presents. Your nonprofit can include your plans with other documentation in a package to illustrate a level of professionalism that the bank or other institution looks for in good risks.

- *Remaining in compliance with federal and state law, particularly those requirements to maintain your nonprofit's 501(c)(3).* The legal and legislative environment has changed dramatically in recent years. With the passage of Sarbanes-Oxley Act of 2002, all organizations, including nonprofits, have been obliged to change the way they do business and accept a higher level of transparency and accountability. Two components of Sarbanes-Oxley are already in place and required of all organizations. Your nonprofit has no excuse for not having a whistleblower policy and a document preservation policy in place.

- *State laws, such as California's Nonprofit Integrity Act, impose other requirements on nonprofits that are either domiciled in California or solicit donations there.* Your nonprofit's risk management plan should address these requirements, and your business continuity plan should include policies and procedures to maintain compliance with fundraising stipulations, particularly if your nonprofit needs to initiate an emergency fundraising campaign.

- *Writing proposals for grants.* Sources of funding, such as foundations and other institutions, are becoming more rigorous in their requirements. Proposals need to include a business plan and should also include risk management and business continuity plans. These funders are to nonprofits what venture capital firms are to private sector companies. They expect to be able to determine if there is a "return" for donated funds in the form of program delivery and solid management practices. Foundation boards want to see results—and want to ensure that funding is going to nonprofits that are economically and institutionally viable.

- *Donors.* Major donors and high-wealth individuals want documented evidence that the nonprofit knows how to manage its operations and the financial assets it oversees. Risk management and business continuity plans, even if presented to a major donor in executive summary form, illustrate the nonprofit's commitment to being good stewards of all donations.

- *Suppliers.* Suppliers and other big-ticket vendors want to be assured that the nonprofit has the capacity to enter into a contract and pay its bills. In addition to any financial statements that might be provided as proof, the existence of a risk management plan and a business continuity plan provides further evidence of good management practices.

- *Auditor.* The nonprofit's auditor will want to review these documents as part of an overall review of the nonprofit's books.

- *Partnering with other nonprofits or with corporations.* In today's business environment, corporations and other nonprofits will want assurances that partnering with your nonprofit does not pose a risk for them. Your nonprofit's risk management and business continuity plans will demonstrate that your organization is committed to being proactive in dealing with risk and the potential for business interruption.

- *Preserving your nonprofit's good name.* Public trust is a very fragile quality that is intangible but can take years to repair if damaged. One of the challenges in risk management is identifying the ways in which your nonprofit's good name or public image could be damaged. Risk management and business continuity planning can facilitate important discussions around this topic and identify those areas that are currently increasing your nonprofit's vulnerability.

- *Making sure your staff, clients, and volunteers are safe.* Risk management and business continuity plans can help your nonprofit identify those areas, locations, and situations that might pose danger for your staff, clients, and volunteers. A risk management plan could also establish procedures around keeping people safe at special events and fundraisers that the nonprofit presents. A business continuity plan can help to solidify your nonprofit's protocols to deal with an array of emergency situations.

- *Public sector agencies.* If your nonprofit has a contract with a public sector agency, the agency may require proof of a risk management and/or business continuity plan.

- *Your nonprofit's information technology specialist.* Your nonprofit's IT specialist needs to review both the risk management and the business continuity plans. The success of the plans hinges on the skillful use of the IT assets within your nonprofit.

How Risk Management and Business Continuity Planning Facilitates Compliance in Today's New Legislative Environment

Risk management and business continuity plans can facilitate activities needed to bring your nonprofit into compliance with the two provisions of Sarbanes-Oxley legislation that apply to nonprofits, as well as any state legislation that might apply. The April 2005 U.S. Senate Finance Committee Hearings chaired by Senator Charles Grassley (R–Iowa) heard testimony from Diana Aviv, chair of the Independent Sector's Panel on the Nonprofit Sector. The panel was convened in 2004 at the request of the Senate Finance Committee, and presented its work to the Grassley Committee in an effort to provide a response to federal proposals aimed at improving charitable governance and accountability. The Independent Sector panel cited eight guiding principles:

1. A Vibrant Nonprofit Sector Is Essential for a Vital America.

2. The Nonprofit Sector's Effectiveness Depends on Its Independence.

3. The Nonprofit Sector's Success Depends on Its Integrity and Credibility.

4. Comprehensive and Accurate Information about the Nonprofit Sector Must Be Available to the Public.

5. A Viable System of Self-Regulation Is Needed for the Nonprofit Sector.

6. Government Should Ensure Effective Enforcement of the Law.

7. Government Regulation Should Deter Abuse without Discouraging Legitimate Charitable Activities.

8. Demonstrations of Compliance with High Standards of Ethical Conduct Should Be Commensurate with the Size, Scale and Resources of the Organization.

On June 22, 2005, the Panel on the Nonprofit Sector gave its recommendations to the U.S. Senate Finance Committee. The 116-page final report provided 120 suggested actions for the Internal Revenue Service, legislators, and charitable organizations. Some of the changes suggested to the IRS were:

- Charities with at least $2 million in total revenue and filing a Form 990 or Form 990PF would be legally required to conduct a yearly financial audit.

- Organizations with $500,000 to $2 million in total revenue would be required to have an independent public accountant review financial statements.

- Charities with less than $25,000 in revenue would face automatic suspension of tax-exempt status if they fail to file an annual notice with the IRS for three consecutive years.

- Chief executive officers, chief financial officers, or the highest-ranking officer would be required to sign tax and information forms.

- The tax-exempt status of organizations that fail to comply with federal filing requirements for two or more consecutive years would be suspended.

- Penalties imposed on individual and corporate tax preparers for omission or misrepresentation of information and/or disregard of rules and regulations would be extended to preparers of Form 990s.

- The requirement for e-filing of Form 990s and allowance for separate attachments would move forward.

- Federal e-filing efforts would be coordinated with states.

- Applications for tax-exempt status would have to be e-filed.

Some of the changes suggested for nonprofits were:

- Adopt and enforce a conflict of interest policy.

- Include people with some financial literacy on its board of directors.

- Create whistleblower protection policies.

The Independent Sector's recommendations for nonprofits are consistent with Sarbanes-Oxley (SOX) compliance and best practices. These requirements and best practices can be easily integrated into your nonprofit's risk management and business continuity plans. Implementing these requirements and best practices can save your nonprofit money and time and, most important, preserve your nonprofit's good name:

- Incorporating SOX best practices reduces the potential that your nonprofit will experience a financial crisis or scandal relating to management malfeasance. The adverse publicity that follows any scandal scenario can have an immediate devastating effect and trigger a crisis. By having a business continuity plan with a crisis communication component, your nonprofit will be better positioned in a crisis to conduct itself in a manner that inspires public trust.

- Implementing the SOX best practices now saves time and money. Although your nonprofit may not be affected by state law, the two provisions of the act apply to all nonprofits.

- Document preservation can be vital in helping your nonprofit to get through potential crisis scenarios, such as having the IRS ask for a document or having to produce documents in the event of litigation.

- If your nonprofit is in California, having a risk management plan in place can facilitate those actions needed to ensure compliance with the provisions of the state's new law. Your nonprofit's business continuity plan would also need to reflect commitment to compliance by incorporating those provisions of the law that address fundraising campaigns.

- Risk management and business continuity plans that incorporate Sarbanes-Oxley best practices produce additional value in strengthening the nonprofit's internal controls and in promoting a solid organizational infrastructure. Both are essential for growth and maintaining stature within the nonprofit sector and in your community. Like strong bones in human beings, a solid infrastructure enables organizations to better sustain the challenges of doing business.

  - Having a risk management and business continuity plan in place also:
    - Facilitates effective board recruitment and orientation practices.
    - Supports accountability of senior management and board. The board and the senior management understand their roles and obligations.

  - Financial statements need to be prepared in a transparent fashion that accurate and honestly reflect the nonprofit's financial position. Other important financial documents, include correctly prepared IRS Form 990s that are submitted on time and in compliance with other regulatory conditions.

  - Sarbanes-Oxley requirements for all businesses and nonprofit include designing a document retention system results in an organized filing system that preserves files and has a storage/archive system that supports easy access and retrieval. Additionally, there needs to be a written policy prohibiting the destruction of documents during an investigation or legal action.

  - Board accountability has been highlighted in Sarbanes-Oxley legislation. This means that all nonprofits need to develop policies on issues such as conflicts of interest, whistleblower protection, and self-dealing as well as a code of ethics that is signed off on by board and senior management.

Leverage your nonprofit's risk management plan to ensure that the organization is in full compliance with IRS requirements and your nonprofit's business continuity planning needs to ensure that important documents are archived. Prior to 2004, the IRS was not as aggressive in ensuring that nonprofits submitted 990s. Many nonprofits continue to be lax in submitting an IRS Form 990 on an annual basis. That's amazing given the heightened level of scrutiny that the IRS has been empowered to employ. Your nonprofit's risk management and business continuity plans have added value as they can be included with your 990 form to indicate that your nonprofit took steps to come into compliance with the two compulsory areas within SOX (whistleblower protection and document preservation) and took steps to adopt governance and management best practices that emerged from the other components of the legislation.

LEVERAGING RISK MANAGEMENT AND BUSINESS CONTINUITY PLANNING TO IMPROVE THE QUALITY OF FORM 990 FILINGS

Most nonprofit executives know that the IRS Form 990 needs to be made available to any member of the public who requests it. In today's world of Internet access, a nonprofit's 990 can be easily accessed on the Web. Nonprofit information sources such as Guidestar (www.guidestar.org) provide information about nonprofit organizations. Many donors and grant makers search Guidestar before making their funding decisions. IRS Form 990s are published on the Guidestar Web page. It is important for your nonprofit to utilize the opportunity provided by Guidestar and other databases to get the message out that your board and senior management have taken steps to ensure your nonprofit's credibility and accountability. Your risk management and business continuity plans can serve as examples of your nonprofit's commitment to financial transparency and management excellence. The more often these plans are updated and refined, the stronger your nonprofit will grow.

SUMMARY

The primary issues in risk management and business continuity planning are raising the nonprofit's awareness of and commitment to reducing the potential for damage and loss. These two planning functions support Sarbanes-Oxley requirements and best practices to improve accountability and transparency. Identify the steps that your board and senior management have taken to address the Sarbanes-Oxley best practices, and connect these steps to your nonprofit's risk management and business continuity planning. The connection should be seamless.

Time is of the essence! Your nonprofit can be leveraging your risk management and business continuity plan while the rest of the nonprofit world is in denial, clueless, whining, or going out of business. Having these plans in place gives your nonprofit a winning edge.

Ten Ways to Jump-Start the Planning Process

O ften the best way to begin risk management or business continuity planning is simply to jump right in. The process for risk management and business continuity planning should never be cumbersome. Here are some methods to help forward the action.

1. The board and senior management need to make a big deal about risk management and /or business continuity planning.

The more vocal and visible the board and senior management can be around risk management and business continuity planning, the less likely such planning will be dismissed as a fad by staff and volunteers. Staff and volunteers need to see how the board and senior management have adopted the best practices of these types of plans and how *they have changed the rewards* for compliance. Staff and volunteers will ignore planning of any sort until and unless they see a clear change in how things are done and what behavior is rewarded—and that there are unpleasant consequences for failing to comply.

2. Use the template as a framework for the first draft of your risk management and/or business continuity plan. Filling in the blanks is a good thing! You can create an effective risk

management and/or business continuity plan regardless of the size of your nonprofit.

The first edition of your risk management and business continuity plan is a triumph. Regard the template as a means of facilitating that first step. Because good risk management and business continuity planning are continuous processes, your nonprofit will see the plans grow and flourish each time they are updated. Soon the plans will reflect a customized approach that addresses your nonprofit's specific profile rather than the parameters of a template.

3. When beginning to plan, recruit a planning team comprised of the nonprofit's "star players" and make sure that this team is given very visible perks, including arranging for others to take part of their workload.

The nonprofit's star players generally bring high levels of competence and enthusiasm to the table. It is particularly important for the board and senior management to trumpet the planning process as well as to visibly reward those individuals who were chosen to serve on the risk management and/or business continuity planning team. A seat on the team needs to become a plum assignment. The more status that can be accorded the team, the better. The perks do not have to be expensive—or even have a cost assigned to them. Prime parking space reserved for team members' use or permission to work at home several days a week sends an unmistakable message.

4. The templates for both plans are designed to be segmented for use in multiple groups. In the preparation for the DIAD sessions, the materials were collected and prepared by various individuals on the planning team or by departments in the nonprofit. The plan will be assembled like a jigsaw puzzle during the DIAD session.

The templates are comprised of distinct sections that can be completed as part of smaller work groups. This feature segments the work into distinct deliverables, which facilitates preparation for the DIAD session. If the nonprofit is a small organization, the work groups can include board members and key volunteers or even outside experts, such as bankers, CPAs, attorneys, or insurance professionals. Emphasize that the DIAD session will present the principles and practices of risk management or business continuity planning. The collective contribution of the work groups will create the plan.

5. Beware of the "Mozart" expectations. The plan that is created at the end of the DIAD session is just the first edition—not the final, perfect product. Only Mozart was able to write a composition perfectly without making any edits. Your team can expect to make modifications at regular intervals.

The planning team needs to focus on the task, but not be burdened with expectations that the plan produced in the DIAD session is perfect. It's never going to be perfect and it's never going to be absolutely finished. The nature of the plan's recurring steps provides ample opportunities for fine-tuning and course correction.

It is particularly important to ensure that the DIAD sessions are not bogged down with excessive analysis and what-if scenarios. Insist that the team focus on the task at hand. The plan that is produced at the end of the DIAD session may not be perfect or all-inclusive, but it is a step forward in addressing risk management or business continuity issues. The emphasis should be on forwarding the action, not creating an encyclopedia.

6. Build in a strictly timed agenda for the DIAD session. Emphasize that the planning will continue on a regular basis, so what is not addressed in the first DIAD session will be addressed in the next session.

The facilitator should be tasked with ensuring that the entire agenda of the DIAD is presented *as timed*. The discussion needs to be monitored to ensure that it does not go over the length of time that is chosen by your planning team. The team leader and the facilitator need to fully comprehend and be able to visualize how the various sections of the template integrate. Because preparation for the session is vital, the deliverables for each work group should be clearly identified.

7. Focus on the larger issues first. Remember, the process is recurring. There will be another opportunity in three to six months to revisit the first draft of the plan and modify it.

It is important to focus the planning team's energy on the larger issues first. For either risk management or business continuity planning, some issues come to the fore in the initial work group meetings and in the DIAD session. Be sure that the team understands that the number of risks or business continuity issues that will be addressed in any given round of planning is limited. Set a workable number and do a good job completing the necessary tasks. If necessary, move up the next round of risk management or business continuity planning.

8. Document what you already have in place and incorporate it into the template. Don't reinvent the wheel!

Your nonprofit may already have in place evacuation plans, lists of vendors, staff contact lists, or other materials that can be dropped into the template. Great! Drop it into the template. Don't waste time trying to tweak it unless it genuinely needs to be updated.

9. Establish milestones for achievement in 30- to 90-day increments. Schedule risk assessment at regular intervals.

The best way to keep the process going is to acknowledge the accomplishments of the team at every juncture. At the end of the planning cycle, review the accomplishments and knowledge that emerged from the process. Could this knowledge facilitate a more efficient or effective approach in the next round?

10. Keep talking about risk management and business continuity planning—walk the walk and talk the talk. Everyone in your

nonprofit is responsible for risk management; keep the topic in front of everyone.

Keeping risk management and business continuity planning in front of the organization is an effective way to incorporate this planning into the nonprofit's organizational culture. Your nonprofit can have an excellent infrastructure regardless of its size, its age, or its budget. Your nonprofit is an important part of your community. Risk management and business continuity planning nourish your organization—these plans grow strong internal controls and give the organization the stamina to weather any adversity. Good luck in your risk management and business continuity planning!

Appendix A

Risk Management Plan for
[Name of Your Nonprofit Organization]

Goals and Objectives (brief overarching goal and short-term objectives)

- Value proposition of the plan (overarching goal)
- How the plan will facilitate better internal controls and systems within the nonprofit
- Short-term objectives of the projects (can also add long-term objectives if these are important to the nonprofit).

The Nonprofit's Profile

- Location and contact information
- Mission
- Programs
- Number of staff at main office
- Number and location of construction projects (if applicable)
- If applicable:
  - Contracts with public or private sector organizations
  - Projects or programs funded by grants
  - Retail facilities

- Commercial properties
- Social services facilities
- Other information relevant to presenting a programmatic profile

Risk Assessment Section

For each of the Nonprofit's organizational areas, what are the risks associated with:

- *Board* (consider risks associated with board membership, deliberations, and governance issues)
  - Board meetings
  - Decision making
  - Conflict of interest issues
  - Appropriate insurance: Directors & Officers Insurance with Employment Practices Liability Insurance included (D&O with EPLI)
  - Other
- *Staffing/Volunteers* (consider risks associated with recruitment, hiring, retention, supervision, and termination of employees and volunteers)
  - Whistleblower protection policy
  - Hiring and termination practices
  - Americans with Disabilities Act compliance
  - Supervisory practices
  - Compensation issues
  - Grievance procedures (for issues other than waste, fraud, and abuse)
  - Other
- *Operations* (consider risks associated with these major functions)
  - Finance
  - Administration
  - Main office and branch office management (if applicable)
  - Economic development (if applicable)
  - Client services and programs

- Information technology, Web site and other technology
- Fundraising and advancement
- Relations with the Public
  - Interaction with the public—public "image" of the nonprofit (e.g., the way staff and volunteers drive the nonprofit's vehicles, hygiene and grooming of the staff and volunteers and their demeanor toward the public)
  - Hosting the public for an open house or an event.
  - Greeting members of the public as they enter the nonprofit or telephone the nonprofit
  - The overall tone of the nonprofit's Web site and other public relations materials

Prioritize the risks that are identified for each of these organizational components. Tier 1 risks are first in line for action. Tier 2 risks could be considered in the next round of risk management planning. The next section outlines the necessary action to deal with the risks.

Risk Treatment: Action Items for Risk Treatment

- Tier 1—First-priority risks (those risks that the nonprofit decides to address first)
  - Resources needed to address these risks
  - Techniques for dealing with each risk
  - Responsibilities and timelines
  - Desired outcomes/ measurements of success
  - Documentation of prior claims, occurrences
  - Summary—risks that will be addressed this year; what will be done; when it will be done; who is responsible for the action

For consideration in the next round of risk assessment (which will take place in three months, six months, or a year):

- Tier 2 risks (second-priority risks)
  - Resources needed to address these risks
  - Techniques for each risk

- Responsibilities and timelines
- Desired outcomes/measurements of success
- Documentation of prior claims, occurrences

Monitoring and Evaluation of Risk Treatment Strategies

- Objectives in treating the first-round risks
- Expected results and evaluative measures

Current Risk Management Plan

Summary of risks selected for this round of risk management plan, including the risk treatments selected, measures of success to be evaluated for each risk treatment, deliverables, deadlines, and name of the individual responsible for the deliverables.

- Summary of training needs and policies to be reviewed.
- Review of previous risk management plan (if applicable) for the purposes of evaluating the success of the risk treatments.

Timetable for the Next Round of Risk Assessment and Risk Treatment

Appendix B

Business Continuity Plan for
[Name of Your Nonprofit] Date
CONTINUUM OF EMERGENCY SITUATIONS

Emegency	Initial Action	Follow-up
Rolling blackout	Turn off all lights and electrical equipment to prevent a power surge when power is restored. Leave 1 light in "on" mode to determine when power is restored. Activate flashlights and battery-operated radios.	Develop list of tasks that do not require computer support, such as filing.
Medical	Call the main desk and request 911 be contacted. Describe the emergency situation. Stay calm and gather available medical information to be given to emergency personnel.	First Aid and CPR Training for staff on an annual basis.

[continues]

(continued)

Fire in another office in building housing your offices.	Alert the main desk and ensure that 911 has been contacted.	Perform head count at gathering site. Report names of individuals not accounted for to firefighting authorities. Cooperate with firefighters and emergency personnel.
Fire	Alert the main desk and ensure that 911 has been contacted. People can call 911 from their cell phones. Exiting the building should be the first action. Remain calm. Note your location on the evacuation map. Move in an orderly fashion toward the stairs and exit the building. Close all doors as you exit. Don't use elevators. Once outside, move away from the building.	Perform head count at gathering site. Report names of individuals not accounted for to the firefighting authorities.
Criminal activity and workplace violence	Alert the main desk or a supervisor.	Report suspicious activity immediately. Take threats of violence seriously and report them to management.
Earthquake	Stay calm, and "duck and cover." Stay clear of tall objects and windows. Stay under cover until the initial shocks have subsided.	Meet in the designated area. Ensure that staff, clients, and others in the office are accounted for. Advise emergency personnel if anyone is missing.

Sample Evacuation Plan

Should it be necessary to evacuate/relocate during an emergency, considered the following information for implementation.

Evacuation Procedures

- Identify stairways, doors, or other emergency exits. [*Identify these for your site.*]

- Establish location where all staff, volunteers, clients, and visitors are to meet so that management team can do a head count. [*Identify a primary meeting place and an alternate meeting place for your site.*]

- Establish protocols to assist police, firefighters, and other emergency personnel.

In the Event of a Fire

Evacuate the building and relocate through stairwells, *not elevators,* to the ground floor.

- Alert all persons and remain calm but move quickly.

- Listen for instructions and report to the designated emergency exits.

- Emergency meeting place: The meeting place should be determined in advance of an emergency.

- Keep clear of the building to avoid falling debris.

- Everyone has to be accounted for before any member of staff, volunteers, visitors, etc. are permitted to leave the area to go home.

In Case of a Power Outage

If you are in the elevator at the time of a power outage, remain calm and follow these instructions:

1. Push the button to sound the buzzer alarm in the elevator.

2. Open the phone box and follow instructions.

First Aid and Emergency Supplies,
Location of Supplies

- Location of first aid kits [list locations of first aid kits]. First aid kits contain: rubbing alcohol, hydrogen peroxide, anesthetic antiseptic ointment, gauze pads, cloth tape, Band-Aids, bandages, cold pack, scissors, tweezers, and aspirin.

    Emergency food supplies and water located at _____

    _____.

- Flashlights located at each workstation.
- Six pairs of heavy-duty gloves for debris removal located at

    _____.

- Three portable radios and batteries located at_____

    _____.

- Identify individuals who will be certified in first aid and/or CPR training.

    _____

    _____

    _____

    _____

    _____

Location of Emergency Phones, Flashlights,
Portable Radios, and Batteries

_____

_____

_____

_____

_____

There Has Been An Emergency Situation at your Nonprofit. What Should You Do?

Ensure that an alarm has been sounded and that staff, volunteers, and clients know that they must evacuate the building. Follow the evacuation plan and exit the building immediately. CALL 911 ONCE YOU HAVE EXITED THE SITE. *[NOTE: Also, determine how to activate fire alarm from outside or without smoke detectors.]*

- Contact one of the following key staff to obtain instructions about when to report back for work and at what location.
- Contact information for your staff. [Need to have a phone tree for site management staff.]
- Contact information for services.

Supervisor Contact Information

Name:_____

Office telephone: _____

Cell phone:_____

Home telephone: _____

Crisis Communication Plan Worksheet.

- List of media contacts
- Designated spokesperson(s)
- Prepared statement
- Strategy for disseminating information

Staff Availability Checklist

Staff Member Name: _____

Department: _____

Active Phone Number: _____

Present Residence Address: _____

Home E-mail: _____

Any injuries to self?   ❏ yes   ❏ no

If yes, nature of injury:

_____

Any injuries to family member?   ❏ yes   ❏ no

If yes, nature of injury:

_____

Any serious damage to property?   ❏ yes   ❏ no

If yes, specify:

_____

Best times to work your shift:

_____

Any time you could not work?   ❏ yes   ❏ no

If yes, specify: Why?

_____

Transportation: Do you have transportation?   ❏ yes   ❏ no

Can you assist others in getting to work?   ❏ yes   ❏ no

Do you need any assistance?   ❏ yes   ❏ no

If yes, specify:

_____

_____

Contacts for Specific Functions at Your Nonprofit

Person	Division	Function

Critical Functions

- Accounting for all of the staff, volunteers, and clients.
    - Ensure status of all staff, volunteers and clients.
- Assessing damage and establishing a logical sequence for repairs (triage).
- Identifying communication patterns (How does the staff communicate with supervisors, board members, hospital, and others?).
- Securing the necessary services (from the supervisor) to meet client needs.
- [Add other functions here]

Critical Function	Necessary Tasks

Depth of Staffing—if applicable

Critical Function	Alternate Staff #1	Alternate Staff #2

Vendors

Have at least the following information available for *each vendor.*

Vendor name _____

Contact person at vendor (include this person's cell phone number)

_____

Phone number of the business _____

Fax number _____

Your nonprofit's account number _____

Name of person and alternate at your nonprofit who is authorized to

place an order _____

Important! Be sure to compile listings of these categories of vendors in addition to other suppliers. Be sure to list your nonprofit's account number or other identifying data on the same sheet as the contact number for each vendor.

- Utilities: phone, gas/oil, water, sewer
- IT, computer supplies, hardware, and software
- Payroll and other vendors of outsourced functions
- Handyman or contractor
- Automotive repair
- Lock and key
- Glass replacement
- Elevator
- 24-hour emergency numbers for the local government

Staff Roster

[This page includes the names and contact information for all staff members.]

Board Roster

[This page includes the names and contact information for all board members.]

Bibliography

Business Continuity Planning, http://b2bcontinuity.com/businesscontinuityplanning .html.

Independent Sector, Panel on the Nonprofit Sector. *Report to Congress and the Nonprofit Sector on Governance, Transparency and Accountability*, Washington, DC, June 2005.

King, Larry. "Interview with Sarah Ferguson, Duchess of York," *Larry King Live,* CNN, November 16, 2001.

Office of the Attorney General, State of California, *FAQ on Nonprofit Integrity Act of 2004,* Sacramento, CA, January 2005.

Office of the Attorney General, State of California, *Summary of Key Provisions of the Nonprofit Integrity Act of 2004,* Sacramento, CA, October 2004.

U.S. Department of Labor, Occupational Safety and Health Administration, OSHA Fact Sheet, "Workplace Violence," 2002

Wallack, Todd. "Nonprofit Advisory Group in Crisis, Management Center Helped Local Agencies," *San Francisco Chronicle,* January 22, 2004.

Wolverton, Brad. "What Went Wrong? Board Actions at Issue at Troubled D.C. United Way," *Chronicle of Philanthropy,* September 4, 2003, p. 27.

Index

501(c)(3)
classification, 3–4
compliance. *See* Nonprofits
maintenance. *See* Nonprofits
990 form. *See* Form 990

A
Accessories, approximation, 114
Accidents, 60
documentation/analysis, 32
number, 32
Accountability
increase. *See* Executive compensation
public sector, expectations, 4
Achievements, milestones
(establishment), 172
Action steps. *See* Risk treatment
Action summary, sample. *See* Risk
management plan
Administration
functional area, 116
functions, 123
determination, 104
operation, 41
All clear signal, 97, 151
American Red Cross (ARC)
Disaster Services, 70
judgment error, 70
leaders, financial information
request, 74
Americans with Disabilities Act, 29

ARC. *See* American Red Cross
Attorney General, audit (filing), 10–11
Audit committee
interaction, 39
requirement, 10
role, 9
Auditors, documents review, 161
Audits, 42
results, 10
Avoidance, 18. *See also* Risk; Risk
treatment

B
Background checks, 27, 40
Backup files, access (experience), 79
Backup person, 112
knowledge, 79
Backup systems, development, 76
Backup vendors, list, 129
Banks
account numbers, 115
codes, 115
confidence, 23
deposits, For Deposit Only status, 42
impact, 160
statements, forwarding, 42
Batteries, location, 182
BCP. *See* Business continuity planning
Best practices, 150. *See also* Sarbanes-
Oxley Act of 2002
educational work, 52

Blackberry, usage, 3, 157
Blaster virus, impact, 72
Blizzards, impact, 71–72
Board of directors
  accountability, 165–166
  agenda/minutes, 40
  authority, 16
  compliance, 25–26
  contact information, 106
  expectations, 21
  family members/spouses,
      presence, 40
  fiduciary obligations, 25, 39
  function, determination, 103
  impact. *See* Business continuity
      planning; Risk management
  independence, 26
  leadership, 89
  meetings, 27
    frequency, 40
  members
    blend, 110
    legal standards, 26–27
    term limits, 39
  personnel inclusion, financial literacy
      ability, 164
  presentation, outline sample, 63
  risk, 25–27
    assessment, 39–40
    association, 176
  risk management plan
    presentation, preparation, 63
    template, usage, 50
  roster, 191
  senior management collaboration,
      4–5
Bomb threats, 142
  impact, 122
  increase, 27
  instructions, 118
Briefings, usage, 136
Buddy system, creation, 150–151
Building
  avoidance, 97, 144
  red tagging, 68, 84

Business
  contingency planning, training. *See*
      Staff; Volunteers
  continuity
    team leader, 121
    training, 141–148
  failure, 78
  functions, determination, 103–106,
      123
  hours, emergency scenario (sample),
      154. *See also* Post-business hours
  information, sources, 122
  operations, resumption, 5, 86–87
    funding sources, 115
    transition, 99–108
Business continuity plan
  active status, 124
  assemblage, 129–130
  benefits, 122, 142
  considerations, 124
  design, 76–77
  drafts, 172
  Executive Edition, 130
  measurement, 157
  placement, 165–166
  preparation, considerations, 83–85
  protocols, 123
  review, 172
  sample, 86–87, 179–191
  SOX best practices, incorporation,
      165
  templates
    design, 170–171
    usage, 83
  update, timetable, 131
  updating, 108
  usage, 80–81
  writing. *See* Nonprofits
Business continuity planning (BCP), 67,
      83
  Board of Directors, impact, 169
  definition, 68–70, 121
  DIAD, 2–3
    session, 109
  discussion, 172–173

drafts, framework, 169–170
educational pieces, 111
impact. *See* Compliance
introduction, 121–124
leveraging, 159–167
preparation worksheets, 113–114
ROI, 159
senior management, impact, 169
session agenda. *See* Done in a Day
team, 84
  assembly, 110
  leader, impact, 131
  template, 124–131
    introduction, 85–108
    table of contents, 125
  training sessions, outline (sample),
    141–142
value proposition, 76–78
Business interruptions
  coverage, 78
  expectation, 68
  identification, 123
  impact, 68
  recovery, 80
  sources, 71–73
    defining, 141–142
Business resumption, 130
  bridge, 99–100
  component, 69
  financing, 84, 102–103, 105
    sources, 103
  plans, knowledge, 78
  process, 100
  recovery cost, estimation, 102–103
  role, 145
  staff, role, 147
  strategies, 128–129

C

California. *See* Nonprofit Integrity
  Act
California Revenue Service, inspection.
  See Form 990
Cell phones
  impact, 72, 114

listing, 92
usage, 151
Census-taking
  cooperation, 96
  requirement, 96, 143, 151
Certified Public Accountant (CPA), 171
  impact, 10. *See also* Financial
    statements
CGL. *See* Comprehensive general
  liability
Chances for Children foundation,
  67–68
Charities
  revenue, filing requirements, 163
  tax-exempt status, suspension, 163
Civil unrest, impact, 71, 122, 141
Claims. *See also* Product liability claims
  documentation, 44, 45, 62
  occurrences, documentation, 44, 45,
    62
Clients
  comments/complaints, tracking, 29
  communication method, 130
  evacuation, 145
  information, receiving, 94
  safety, 24
    assurance, 161–162
  services, 145
    function, determination, 104
Comments/complaints, tracking. *See*
  Clients
Committee setup, 20
Community-wide disaster, preparation,
  79–80
Compensation, excess, 61
Compliance. *See* Board of directors;
  Federal law; Nonprofits; State
  law
  facilitation
    business continuity planning,
      impact, 162–166
    risk management, impact, 162–166
  rewards, change, 169
Comprehensive general liability (CGL)
  policy, 31

Computer viruses, 122, 142
Conflict of interest, 39
    policy, 9
        adoption/enforcement, 164
Contact information, 92
Contingency planning
    assumptions, 4–6
    overview, 1–4
Continuity training. *See* Business
Contracts, loss (impact), 72
Corporate tax preparers, penalties
        (imposition), 163–164
Corporations, partnering, 23–24
    importance, 161
CPA. *See* Certified Public Accountant
CPR training, 144
Crime, impact, 72–73
Criminal activity, 57, 92
    BCP, sample, 180
Criminal acts, impact, 72–73
Crisis
    communication planning, 74
    occurrence, action plan, 75–76
    recurrence, 74
Crisis communication plan, 73–76
    basics, 74–76
    usage, 90–95
    worksheet, 184
Crisis incident, nonprofit reaction,
        95–97, 142–148
Crisis incident management, 129–130
    component, 69
    knowledge, 78
    leadership, 89
    role, 145
    strategies, 86
    transition, 99–108
    usage, 88–89, 124–126
Crisis incident strategies, 89–99
Crisis Management Team leader,
        announcement, 93
Crisis management team staffing, 93
Critical functions, 105, 187
    disruption, 80
    resumption. *See* Operations

Cross-functional team, creation, 122
Curriculum, design. *See* Training

D
Damage, extent (determination), 98–99
Data dump, 110
Data files, remote access, 124
Databases
    backup
        assurance, 129
        process, frequency, 114
    theft, 74
Deadline items, reports, 106
Debris, avoidance, 97
Decision making, compression, 2–3
Deliverables, 109
    description, 124
    examples, 59
    focus, 131
Desktop
    computers, number, 114
    exercises, 152–157
        participation, 153
        setup/process, 153–154
        success, measurement, 156–157
    simulation, 124
Discrimination, claims (prevention), 29
Documents
    disposal, protocol, 8
    location, 106
    management/preservation
        policy, 8–9
    preservation, 164, 166
        importance, 8
        policy, 42
    retention policy. *See* Sarbanes-Oxley
        Act of 2002
Done in a Day (DIAD)
    business continuity planning session
        agenda, 121
    date, selection, 53, 118
    method, 2. *See also* Business
        continuity planning; Risk
        management
    template, usage, 5–6

preparation, timetable frame, 112–116
template, usage, 111
Done in a Day (DIAD) session, 19,
    54–64, 120–131. *See also*
    Business continuity planning;
    Risk management
  agenda, sample, 55
  conclusion, 51
  conducting, process, 55–59
  expectations, 171
  feedback/input, 50
  format, sample, 55, 121–124
  one week prior preparation, 53,
    118–119
  planning, quality, 50, 111
  plans, assembly, 170–171
  preparation, 53–54
    process, 49–54, 109–120
    timetable, usage, 51–54
  presumption, 5
  summary/Q&A, 58–59
  three weeks prior preparation, 51–52,
    112–113
  timed agenda, 171–172
    importance, 54
  two weeks prior preparation, 52–53,
    113–114
Donors
  information, requirement, 161
  loss, impact, 72
Doors, identification, 95
Drucker, Peter, 159
Drug/alcohol abuse, prohibition, 41

E
Earthquakes, 92, 122, 141
  BCP, sample, 180
  impact, 71–72
Electrical power, loss (impact), 71, 122,
  142
Electronic files
  access, 84
  backup
    assurance, 129
    frequency, 114

Electronic resources, access, 104
Electronic storage, 106
  usage, 137
Elevators, alarms (sounding), 97
Eligibility requirements, 42
E-mail
  addresses, alternatives, 118
  backup, 129
  considerations, 8
  function, determination, 104
Emergency
  calm, importance, 143
  contact numbers, 106
  evacuation exercises, process/setup,
    149–150
  exits, identification, 95
  financial protocols, 116
  fundraising, 97–98
    component, 69
    involvement, 99
  meeting place, 143
  nonprofits plan, 144–145
  occurrence, 78–79
  preparation, nonprofit commitment,
    148
  preparedness
    exercises, nature/use, 148–149
    success, measurement,
      156–157
  responders, impact, 95
  scenario
    creation, 154
    impact. *See* Offices
    sample. *See* Business; Post-business
      hours; Workplace
  situations
    continuum, 91–92, 179–191
    nonprofit reaction, 183
    strategies, 90
  supplies, location, 144
    sample, 182
  telephones
    calls, routing, 54, 120
    location, 152
    numbers, list, 130

Emergency donations
  acceptance/processing procedures, 98
  acknowledgment, procedures, 98
  conduit, 92
Employees, accountability/performance
      expectations, 40
Entity, viability, 77
Equipment, impact, 105–106
Ethical conduct, standards, 163
Evacuation. *See* Clients; Staff; Visitors;
      Volunteers
  exercises, process/setup. *See*
      Emergency
  planning, 95–97
  plans, 118
    sample, 95–97, 181–182
  procedures, 142, 181. *See also* Fire;
      Power outage
Executive compensation, accountability
      (increase), 11
Executive function, determination, 103
Executive summary, 55, 121
Executive team members, loss (impact),
      72

F

Facilitator
  briefing, 53
  commitment, 54
  engagement, 112–113
  impact, 124
  steps, 58–59
  usage, 51
Family
  emergency preparedness, 85
  member
    injury, 102
    presence. *See* Board of directors
Federal e-filing efforts, state
      coordination, 164
Federal law, compliance, 23
  continuation, 160
Feedback, providing, 22, 111
FEMA, response, 88
Ferguson, Sarah, 67–68

Files, location, 106
Finance operations, 41
  function, determination, 104
Financial databases, corruption (impact),
      72, 122, 142
Financial discrepancies, impact, 30
Financial institutions
  confidence, 23
  impact, 160
  information, receiving, 94–95
Financial mismanagement, 57
Financial objectives, 24
Financial operations, 117
Financial professional, 60
  feedback, 50
  input, 111
Financial reviews, 42
Financial statements, preparation, 165
  auditing, CPA (impact), 11
Financing, sources. *See* Business
      resumption
Fire
  BCP, sample, 180
  drills, 150–151
  evacuation procedures, 181
  impact, 71, 142
  nonprofits, reaction, 143–144
  occurrence, 91
  protocol, 96–97
First aid supplies, location, 90,
      118, 144
  sample, 182
Fiscal mismanagement, 73
Flashlights, location, 90, 144, 152, 182
Flipchart (flip chart), usage, 53, 119,
      120, 128
Floods, impact, 71–72, 122, 141
Form 990
  California Revenue Service
      inspection, 1
  e-filing requirement, 164
  filing, 163
    quality, improvement, 166–167
  Internal Revenue Service
      inspection, 1

preparations, 165
  detal/accuracy enhancement, 9
  submitting, 25
Form 990PF, filing, 163
Functions, 126–128
  examples, 123
Funding source. *See* Business
  problems, 72
Fundraising
  activities, 11–12
  component. *See* Emergency
  function, determination, 104
  operations, 41

G

Government regulations, impact, 163
Grants, proposals (writing), 23, 160–161
Grassley, Charles, 1, 70
  hearings, findings, 4
Growth, facilitation, 1–2
Guidestar, 166

H

Hands-on training exercises, 148–157
Hazardous materials event, 118
Healy, Bernadine, 70
Hidden barriers, awareness, 50, 110–111
Human resources
  functional area, 116
  functions, 123
    determination, 104
  HR decision, 149
  litigation, 57
  management issues, 27
Hurricane Katrina
  aftermath, 88
  impact, 71, 79–80
Hurricanes
  impact, 71–72, 116
  staff availability checklist, sample, 146

I

Ignorance, impact, 21
Incident management. *See* Crisis
  incident management

Independent Sector, guiding principles,
  162–163
Individual tax preparers, penalties
  (imposition), 163–164
Information. *See* Restricted information
  assemblage, 49–50, 110
  sources. *See* Business
Information technology (IT)
  functional area, 116
  functions, 123
    determination, 104
  infrastructure, 113–114, 130
    usage, 84
  operations, 41
  precedence, 103
  professional, feedback/input, 50
  specialist, review, 162
  systems, 104
  vendors. *See* Primary IT vendors
Infrastructure problems, impact, 71
In-service sessions, 136
Inspection, risk area, 29
Instant messaging, considerations, 8
Instructions. *See* Staff; Volunteers
  following, ability, 156
Insurance
  broker, interaction, 21
  claims, 52, 56
    documentation, 32
    number, 32
  coverage, 78
  impact, 159
  portfolio, management, 15–16
  premiums, reduction, 81
  professional
    contact, 105
    feedback/input, 50, 111–112
    partnership, 23
    purchase, 20
Internal controls, 32–33
Internal Revenue Service
  actions, suggestions, 163–164
  inspection. *See* Form 990
  problems, 57
  tax-exempt classification, 17

Internet access, function
    (determination), 104
Intranet training, 137

L

Laptops
  impact, 114
  usage, 53, 119, 120
LCD projector, usage, 54, 119, 120
Legal environment, changes (overview),
    6–12
Legal professional, feedback/input, 50
Liberty Fund, 70
Location. *See* Workplace
Losses, frequency/severity, 32

M

Management. *See* Risk management
  functions, 104
  transparency, 9
Materials
  destruction, 8
  impact, 105–106
  theft, 72–73
  types, usage, 113
  usage. *See* Spokespersons
Media
  contacts, 93–94, 145
  interest, leveraging, 98
  relations, 93–95
Medical emergencies, 91
  BCP, sample, 179
Meeting location, specification, 95
Metrics
  establishment. *See* Results
  usage. *See* Risk management
Mismanagement. *See* Financial
    mismanagement; Fiscal
    mismanagement
  impact, 30
Modification. *See* Risk; Risk treatment
  usage, 18
Morgan Stanley, terrorist attack,
    67, 148
Mozart expectations, 171

N

Natural disasters, impact, 71–72
Negative loss, 38
Nolan, Tom, 15
Noncompliance. *See* Sarbanes-Oxley
    Act of 2002
Nonprofit Integrity Act (California), 4,
    10–12
  requirements, imposition, 160
Nonprofit risk management
  assumptions, 4–6
  overview, 1–4
Nonprofits
  501(c)(3)
    compliance, 160
    maintenance, 23, 160
  800 number, usage, 92
  assistance, 94
  business continuity plan
    benefit, 80
    discussion, 147
    writing, 80
  California operations, 10–12
    risk management plan, impact, 165
  changes, 33
    suggestions, 164
  charity collection, 74
  compliance, 8
  evacuation plans, editing, 117–120
  expectations. *See* Staff; Volunteers
  functions, contacts, 186
  identity, 3–4
  interests, 3
  internal controls, 37
  internal structure, strengthening, 1–2
  legal status, problem, 17
  mission, 75, 80
  name, preservation, 24, 145, 161
    value proposition, 76–77
  name, safety, 138
  needs, identification, 129
  offices, destruction (assumption), 127
  operations
    information, 116–117
    resumption, staff training, 145, 147

partnering, 23–24
  importance, 161
plan, 144–145. *See also* Emergency
policies/procedures
  development, 7
  enforcement, 40
profile, 38, 175–176
provisions, 10–12
reaction. *See* Crisis incident;
      Emergency; Fire; Power outage
reputation, 43
  preservation, 145
sector
  effectiveness/success, 162
  information, accuracy, 163
  self-regulation, need, 163
  star players, recruitment, 170
structure, risk management (impact),
      16–17
thumbnail sketch, 38
web site, usage, 92, 94
Nonprofits risk
  areas, 25–30
  avoidance process, explanation, 130
  impact, 57
  management plan, 175–178
    assembly, process, 58
    table of contents, 36–37

O
Occupational Safety and Health
      Administration (OSHA), advice.
      See Workplace violence
Occurrences. *See* Claims
Offices, emergency scenario (impact), 84
Online donations, security, 98
Operational databases, corruption
      (impact), 72, 122, 142
Operational priorities, 105
Operations
  critical functions, resumption, 128
  description, 17
  resumption, 79. *See also* Business
    process, 129
    strategies, 145

risk, 29–30
  assessment, 41–42
  association, 176–177
Organizational behavior, knowledge, 51
Organizational change, introduction
      process, 63
Organizational efficiency, level, 157
Organizational systems/procedures,
      transparency, 76
Organizations
  tax-exempt status, compliance
      (failure), 163
  understanding, 76
Outsourced functions, vendor
      information, 114–115
Oxley, Michael, 6

P
PalmPilot, usage, 3, 157
Panel on the Nonprofit Sector,
      recommendations, 163–164
Paper-only records, protection, 118,
      130, 145
Paralysis by analysis, 2–3
Payroll
  function, determination, 104
  priority, 105
  questions, 117
Perquisites
  usage, 54, 119
  value, 110
Personal digital assistants (PDAs)
  impact, 72, 106, 114
  usage, 157
Person-made interruptions, 122, 142
Phones. *See* Telephones
PipeVine, donations (siphoning), 74
Planning. *See* Business contingency
      planning; Business continuity
      planning
  process, jumpstarting, 5–6, 169
Police action, 122, 141
Portable radios, location, 144, 152, 182
Post-business hours, emergency scenario
      (sample), 154–155

Power outage, 90
  drills, 151–152
  evacuation procedures, 181
  nonprofits reaction, 144
  protocol, 97
Preparedness exercises, nature/use. *See* Emergency
Pre-session collaboration, 5
Press release, importance, 93
Primary IT vendors, 113
Prioritization. *See* Risk
Priority risks, 59
Private sector
  contacts, 106
  lessons, 78–81
Product liability claims, 57
Programmatic expansion, 24
Programs operation, 41
Project Open Hand, 15
Projects, short-term objectives, 37–38
Protocols, establishment, 96
Public
  information, receiving, 94
  risk, association, 177
Public perception, tainting, 88
Public relations, 17, 30, 145
  functional area, 116
  risk assessment, 43
Public sector
  agencies, 162
  contacts, 106
  expectations. *See* Accountability
Public trust
  fragility, 24, 161
  maintenance, 70, 74
Publicity, impact, 25, 56, 73

R
Radios. *See* Portable radios
Reception staff, briefing, 53
Recording secretary, designation, 53–54, 119
Recordkeeping, risk area, 29
Records, information, 115

Recovery cost, estimation. *See* Business resumption
Red Cross. *See* American Red Cross
Remote access, usage, 84
Resource needs, identification, 124
Restricted information, 115
Results, monitoring, 18–19. *See also* Risk management
  definition, 57
  metrics, establishment, 58
Retention, 18. *See also* Risk; Risk treatment
Return on investment (ROI), 159. *See also* Business continuity planning; Risk management
Riots, 122, 141
Risk. *See* Priority risks; Tier 1 risks; Tier 2 risks
  addressing, 61
  areas
    considerations, 60
    identification, 47, 136
    selection, 46
  association. *See* Board of directors; Operations; Public; Staffing; Volunteers
  avoidance, 31, 44, 139
    process, explanation. *See* Nonprofits risk
  identification, 30–32
  interaction, 139–140
  level, 18
  modification, 31, 45, 140
  prioritization, 43–45
  resources, 44
  retention, 31, 44, 139–140
  strategy, 36, 139
  transfer, 31, 45, 140
Risk assessment, 18, 25, 38–43. *See also* Board of directors; Operations; Public relations; Staff; Volunteers
  components, 176–177
  definition, 56
  explanation, 139
  implementation components, 24–25

process, 58
review/selection, 59–60
    continuation, 60
scheduling, 172
timetable, 178
Risk management, 15–19
administration/monitoring, 139
appearance, 21–22
benefits, 24
Board of Directors, impact, 169
deferment, 21
definition, 15, 56, 138–139
    exclusion, 19–21
DIAD, 2–3
    method, 2
    session, 49
discussion, 172–173
drafts, framework, 169–170
engagement, 2
evaluation, 57
holistic process, 22
impact. See Compliance; Nonprofits
implementation components,
    24–25
leveraging, 159–167
methods
    identification, 45
    selection, 61–62
myths, 2–4
primary method, 61
process, 33
    explanation, 139
resources, listing, 45
ROI, 159
role, 141
senior management, impact, 169
steps, 17
strategy, 31, 61–62
    implementation, 18
    results, monitoring, 32–33
    selection, 44
team, assemblage, 49
template
    results (monitoring), metrics
        (usage), 47

usage, 35
usage, benefits, 57
training. See Staff; Volunteers
agenda, 137–140
session
    objectives, 138
    outline, sample, 138–140
understanding, 21–22
value-added aspect, 23–24
Risk management activities, 17–19, 27,
    140
continuation, 16
definition, 56–57
implementation, 30–34, 139
organization, 35, 37
rounds, frequency, 47
scheduling, 33–34
timetable
    scheduling, 58
    usage, 47
Risk management plan
achievement schedule, 38
action summary, sample, 62
construction, 37–47
current form, 178
drafts, 172
goals/objectives, 37–38, 175
ongoing process, 22
placement, 165–166
preparation, 77–78
presentation, preparation. See Board
    of directors
review, 172
sample, 175–178
short-term objectives, 175
SOX best practices incorporation,
    165
summary, 37, 140
table of contents. See Nonprofits risk
templates
    design, 170–171
    electronic version, 63
    usage. See Board of directors; Staff;
        Volunteers
value proposition, 37

Risk management planning, 24–30
  deferment, 2
  inclusion, 22
  steps, 58
  timetable, 59
  training curriculum outline, 56–58
Risk manager, role, 15–16
Risk treatment
  action items, 177–178
  action steps, 45–46
    identification, 58
  assignments, sample summary, 46
  avoidance, 56
  modification, 56–57
  retention, 56
  selection, 58
  strategies, 44, 61
    compilation, 62
    monitoring/evaluation, 178
    sample summary, 46
  techniques, 19
  timetable, 178
  transfer, 57
Rolling blackout, 91
  BCP, sample, 179

S
Safety
  equipment, 90
  importance, 84, 129
Sarbanes, Paul, 6
Sarbanes-Oxley Act of 2002 (SOX)
  best practices, 9–10, 164–166
    implementation, 3, 164
    incorporation, 164, 165. *See also*
      Business continuity plan; Risk
      management plan
  compliance, 60, 164–166
  document retention policy, 26
  legislation, application, 162
  noncompliance, 57
  obligations, 7
  passage, 23, 160
  requirements, 77, 165
Second-priority risks, 37, 44–45

Security access information, 115
Self-efficacy, level, 141
Self-regulation, need. *See* Nonprofits
Senior management
  collaboration. *See* Board of directors
  impact. *See* Business continuity
    planning; Risk management
September 11 (2001), lessons, 67–68
Server, presence, 114
Sexual harassment, prohibition, 41
Short-term objectives. *See* Projects
Signatories, requirements, 42
Signature authority, 115
Skills
  demonstration, 137
  testing, before/after quizzes, 137
Software
  backup, 129
  impact, 105–106
  purchase, 20–21
Solicitation campaign, commencement,
  11
SOX. *See* Sarbanes-Oxley Act of 2002
Spokespersons
  materials, usage, 75
  media inquiries, direction, 99
  statements, 93
  usage, 75
Spouses, presence. *See* Board of
  directors
Sprinklers, zones (division), 71
Staff
  availability checklist, 100–102
    sample, 101, 185. *See also*
      Hurricanes
  blend, 110
  complaints, number, 32
  contact information, 106
  contingency planning, training, 135
  cross-training, 118, 130
  discipline/termination protocols, 41
  e-mail, usage, 100
  evacuation, 145
  instructions, 151
  job descriptions, 41

members
assistance, 102
injuries, 100
loss, impact, 72
property, damage, 102
morale, 32
nonprofit expectations, 89, 99
phone number, usage, 100
residence address, usage, 100
resources, 16
risk, 27–29
assessment, 40–41
risk management
plan template, usage, 50
training, 135
role. *See* Business resumption
roster, 190
safety, 24
assurance, 161–162
status, 145
training. *See* Nonprofits
transportation, usage, 102
work, inability, 102
Staffing
depth, 105, 127
emphasis, 80
list, 188
measurement, 157
risk, association, 176
Stairways, identification, 95, 96
Stakeholders
communication, 94–95, 145
confidence, preservation, 77–78
Star players, recruitment. *See*
Nonprofits
State law
compliance, 23
continuation, 160
requirements, imposition, 160
State legislation, example, 10–12
Street closures, impact, 71
Success
outcomes/measurements, 44, 61
listing, 45
Supervisor contact information, 183

Suppliers
assurance, 161
dependence, 85

T

Tax preparers, penalties (imposition).
See Corporate tax preparers;
Individual tax preparers
Tax-exempt status
applications, e-filing requirement, 164
suspension. *See* Charities
Telecommunications infrastructure,
113–114
Telephones
calls, routing. *See* Emergency
location, 182
system description/vendor, 114
tree, 92
Templates
design. *See* Business continuity plan;
Risk management plan
information, incorporation, 172
introduction. *See* Business continuity
planning
results. *See* Risk management
table of contents. *See* Business
continuity planning
usage, 5–6. *See also* Board of
directors; Business continuity
plan; Done in a Day; Risk
management; Staff; Volunteers
Tier 1 risks, 60, 177
Tier 2 risks, 60, 177–178
Timed agenda. *See* Done in a Day
session
Time-limited scenarios, usage, 152–153
Timetable
establishment, 108
usage. *See* Done in a Day session;
Risk management activities
Training
agenda/curricula, sample, 138–148
curriculum, design, 136–138
exercises. *See* Hands-on training
exercises

Training (Continued)
    leveraging, 135–136
    practice, 149–152
    strategies, 63
Transfer. See Risk; Risk treatment
    option, 18
Transportation, availability, 102
Travel claims
    payment guidelines, 42
    review, 61

U

United Way, financial reports (changes),
    74
U.S. Senate Finance Committee
    hearings, 1
    recommendations, 163–164
Users manuals, 147

V

Value proposition. See Risk
    management plan
Vehicles, information, 115
Vendors, 106–107
    categories, 107
    dependence, 85
    impact, 87
    information. See Outsourced
        functions
        availability, 189
        receiving, 94
Viruses. See Blaster virus; Computer
    viruses
Visitors, evacuation, 145
Volunteers
    blend, 110
    business contingency, training, 135
    complaints, number, 32
    discipline/termination protocols, 41
    evacuation, 145
    information, receiving, 94
    instructions, 151

job volunteers, 41
morale, 32
nonprofit expectations, 89, 99
resources, 16
risk
    assessment, 40–41
    association, 176
risk management
    plan template, usage, 50
    training, 135
safety, 24
assurance, 161–162

W

Web site
    access, function (determination), 104
    usage. See Nonprofits
Web-based training, 137
What-if scenarios, 171
Whistleblower protection, 7, 166
    adherence, 6
Whistleblower protection policies
    absence, 60
    creation, 164
    presence, 40
Work activities, concepts/practices
    (integration), 138
Workplace (location)
    alternatives, 87
        working, 107–108
    emergency scenario, sample, 155–156
Workplace (location) violence, 92, 149
    BCP, sample, 180
    drill, 152
    impact, 72
    increase, 27
    OSHA advice, 28–29
World Trade Center, terrorist attack, 67
Worms, infestation, 122, 142

Z

Zerbe, Dean, 1